The Newlyweds' Guide to
SETTING UP HOME

The Newlyweds' Guide to
SETTING UP HOME
creating an affordable and stylish first home

Gail Abbott

CICO BOOKS
LONDON NEW YORK

Published in 2009 by CICO Books
An imprint of Ryland Peters & Small Ltd

20–21 Jockey's Fields   519 Broadway, 5th Floor
London WC1R 4BW   New York, NY 10012

www.cicobooks.com

10 9 8 7 6 5 4 3 2 1

Text © Gail Abbott 2009
Design and photography © CICO Books 2009

A CIP catalog record for this book is available from the Library of Congress
and the British Library.

ISBN 978 1 906525 73 6

Printed in China

Editor: Gillian Haslam
Designer: Luis Peral Aranda

CONTENTS

GETTING STARTED

Moving into your first home as a couple is a new experience, exciting and thrilling and full of expectations for a life together, but it can feel daunting too. It's a dream come true for you both, but now here you are, with a bare apartment or house to turn into your dream home. You may be looking at undecorated walls or—even worse—old-fashioned carpets and wallpaper, a kitchen that's seen better days, and a bathroom that looks like a place to wash and run, and wondering how on earth you are going to transform these rooms into a cool, stylish home where you can relax, cook, and entertain. You'd like your new home to be a sanctuary that will welcome you as you step through the door at night, where you can invite friends to eat and stay over, and where you can chill out at weekends. Home is the one place where you can be exactly who you are, where you can express your personality and enthusiasms in the style of furniture you buy, the colors you choose, and the things you put on display.

CREATING A HOME

Home should be a place to comfort and nurture ourselves, but if you have a limited budget, decorating and furnishing an entire house or apartment is a tall order. This book will help you to find ways to save money by mixing second-hand buys with chain-store flat-pack furniture or hand-me-downs and still get a stylish look. There are lots of inspirational ideas too, for upgrading your kitchen and bathroom without a lot of expense, but if you can find the money to tear it all out and start from scratch, there are guidelines to help you pick the most economical kitchen solutions or design a budget bathroom that looks fabulous, as well as lots of planning tips.

Inspire yourself

If you have been living in your family home up until now, you will have been sheltered from making decisions about decorating, apart perhaps from your own bedroom. Or you may have been sharing an apartment or house with friends where there was little room for individuality beyond putting up a few posters and dreaming of the day when you could have free rein. You might already have set up home for yourself, living in your own rented apartment where you could begin to develop your own style and get to know what you like and dislike.

Joining forces

Bringing two lives together and combining furniture and possessions you already own will take a lot of discussion and sharing of ideas. It's a great way to learn about each other, but one for which you will both need to develop ways of listening. You are two individuals who need to have spaces to share and spaces to be yourself. In a small home this might involve zoning areas of the living room or the bedroom, perhaps a section of the living room for computer games or playing music and a table in the bedroom for a creative activity. In the chapter on Dual-Purpose Rooms on page 143, you'll find lots of ideas for squeezing in a home office or an art table, and for places to make up a spare bed for overnight guests.

Running your own place involves a certain amount of organization and planning if all the mundane details are to be kept under control, such as the bills needing to be paid on time, the garbage put out, and floors kept clean, but it also gives you lots of scope for creativity and generosity. Sharing responsibilities—such as deciding who cleans the bathroom and who does the food shopping—is the nitty gritty of life. Welcoming friends and family, cooking together, and relaxing in front of a movie is your down-time, when you can enjoy what you have achieved in your own beautiful, stylish, and individual home.

THE BARE BASICS

Before you can make decisions like choosing colors, picking curtains, or buying furniture, take a good look around your new home and ask yourself the following questions.

Where to start

- What interesting features are already there?
- Do the rooms look small or dark?
- Do we have pretty cornices, alcoves, beautiful windows, or a lovely fireplace that can be turned into a focus?
- Perhaps there are no interesting details? Are the rooms square and boxy, with no alcoves or decorative moldings?
- How much storage do we have? Are there built-in closets, cupboards under the stairs, or enough shelves? Is there enough space to store all our stuff? Where will we put the vacuum cleaner and the ironing board?
- What colors are on the walls right now? Are they plain white, magnolia, or a strong color?
- Do we like the color that's there, or would we like to redecorate?

- Can we keep the floor coverings or will we need to replace or remove them?
- What's the lighting like? Are there bare bulbs hanging from every ceiling, recessed lighting, or wall lights?
- Do we need to make changes to the bathroom, like a new suite, tiles, or floor?
- Do we need to update the kitchen?
- If not, can we simply change the wall color and make the most of what we've already got?
- What have we collected between us?
- Do we have a view we'd like to look at, or one we'd rather disguise?
- What furniture have we been given or already have, and do we like it?

Making the most of what you have

Now go through your new home systematically, making a note of all the pros and cons of every room. Be practical, and don't think about the look of it at this stage. Concentrate on what you can live with, and what you can't and whether each room has the basics you need to live efficiently and comfortably. This will help you build up a clear picture in your mind about what you need to do.

Why not try?

- Drawing a rough plan of each room and putting down the measurements. Include all the doors, windows, radiators, and any fireplace or alcoves you have too. This will help you work out where you can fit in the furniture later.
- Taking digital snaps of all the rooms as a record of how it all looked before you started.

A bland bedroom

Plus: there's plenty of natural daylight from the window in this bedroom.

Minus: it's a tiny room with an odd shape that makes it difficult to know where to place the furniture.

What you can do:

• Build a customized storage unit that is designed to fit the unusual shape and provides a flat wall for the bed.

• Paint all walls in a soft white to minimize the different angles and the ceiling white to reflect even more light.

A small kitchen

Plus: there's not much to recommend in a kitchen this small.

Minus: there's no natural daylight except from the adjoining room, and hardly any storage or cooking space.

What you can do:

• Keep the units white and choose glass-fronted wall cabinets that will increase the sense of space.

• Fit built-in appliances that will use the space most effectively.

• Get lighting from strip lights under the wall units.

• Fit "metro" style, white glossy tiles above the work surface to reflect as much light as possible.

A bare living room

Plus: a contemporary living space in a loft-style apartment with brick walls, long windows, and a dark-stained wooden floor.

Minus: the room looks bare and unwelcoming and the white-painted walls give it a cold feeling. With no alcoves, there is no obvious place to build a set of bookshelves.

What you can do:

• Find unusual metal wall shelving that fits in with the industrial feel of the apartment and use them for displaying colorful books that will bring life and color to the walls.

• Break up the large, anonymous space by arranging furniture away from the walls in groups that will make more intimate areas.

Left: Make a finished inspiration board with scraps of wallpaper, fabrics, trims, and accessories, like this romantic scheme for a bedroom. The combination of rose pink with blue and white stripes is given a lift with shiny beads and embroidered braid.

Below: Make a start by collecting anything that catches your eye and pin them up together on your inspiration board; a green and cream soap wrapper, a length of pink printed fabric, a card hand, and a black-and-white magazine page have no common link, but together they begin to build into a feeling of color and texture.

Inspire yourself

There's such a fantastic choice of decorating styles to choose from that when you're setting up home you could be forgiven for not knowing where to start! Country, contemporary, retro, vintage, or ethnic-inspired—these are just a few of the ways you can go. If you are confused and not sure what you like, don't panic. You can only get to know your own taste by looking around and making a collection of images that inspire you and give you a direction to follow.

Start by collecting photos, fabrics, paint swatches, and anything else that catches your eye. Get yourself a pin board and start ripping out magazine pictures, pick up postcards from exhibitions, take your own photos when you're out and about. Anything that interests you can go in the mix, such as pictures of furniture and accessories from catalogs, travel pictures, swatches of fabric. If your cuttings overflow the board, start keeping them in a folder and pin the best up together. Keep adding and taking away. You'll soon get a feel for the type of look you want to create.

Style ideas board

To spark your imagination, collect and display:
- An image that represents the way you feel about your home
- Fabric samples
- Paint color samples
- Magazine room sets
- Images of furniture
- Flooring ideas
- Photos of window treatments
- Finishing touches to complete the scheme

WHAT'S YOUR STYLE

Feeling inspired? Now is the time to begin looking at the style of your new home and making some decisions on the overall look you want to go for. Whether you are moving into a high rise apartment in the city or a tiny cottage in the country; a small bungalow in the suburbs or a wooden chalet by the sea, the style of the house will to some extent dictate the way you decorate. But there's no reason why you can't fit a minimal, modern feel into an old house, or why you shouldn't create a retro look in a new space. Your home is where you will be revived and restored, it's a place that will say everything about you and your lifestyle, so you'll want to create a home that reflects your character and personality. Are you a cool, organized type, or a wild child who likes to surround herself with color and pattern? Do you love the comfort of soft textures and country flowers or are you a keen bargain-hunter who loves to spend Sundays at the flea market? Bear your own personal traits in mind when choosing a style.

Top tips

• Choose your style and be strict with yourself. A collection of "themed" rooms that don't have a common identity will be confusing and messy. Much better to have one simple or classic look that gently leads you from one room to another.

• Be careful about buying ethnic artefacts when traveling to other countries, unless they fit in with your look. That Moroccan lamp might look great in the souk, but might not be so much at home in your country-style living room..

Contemporary

Clean lines with reflective surfaces will always say contemporary style, a look that suits anyone who loves cutting edge design. A smoked glass coffee table, a boxy shelf unit, and an unfussy sofa in shades of monochrome add up to a modern look that relies on a minimal approach.

Country

White walls, stripped floorboards, an easy chair with baggy slipcover, a wood-burning stove with logs in baskets—these are all the basic elements of an easy country style for anyone who loves the simple life.

Retro

This is a look that speaks volumes about your individuality and a keen nose for hunting out a bargain. This is a fashionable style that can be expensive—but can be put together on a budget if you seek out 50s and 60s furniture on eBay.

There's no need to spend a fortune in expensive stores—furnish your home with style by knowing what you are looking for in second-hand stores or on eBay.

Once you have found the decorating style that suits you, you will discover that you start to seek out accessories, fabrics, cushions, and lamps everywhere you go.

Classic

If you haunt the high street at sale time you will be on the right track for creating a classic look in your new home. Simple lines and uncomplicated styling are easily found if you keep to the basics. Add a splash of color and put it all together with lashings of fresh white for a budget look.

Oriental

For the wild child who loves color and pattern this ethnic-inspired look is perfect. Keep a riot of color within bounds with an emphasis on oriental fabrics, colorful glass, and beads. Look in dress fabric stores for lengths of woven textiles with a shine and a shimmer.

Vintage

The vintage look is based on old pieces that you might find in a thrift store or charity shop, or have been handed down from your great aunt, but you don't need to fill your home with old furniture. Find a faded piece of fabric to make into a pillow for a modern chair, or place a vintage lamp on a side table and get the vintage style in minutes.

THE MAIN ELEMENTS

Once you've decided which direction you are heading in, it's a good idea to consider the main elements that any comfortable and practical room will need. This chapter sets out some of the basics that need to be coordinated to bring it all together. Lighting and storage are the first things to think about—the most beautifully decorated room will look bland and flat without good lighting, and there's no point having a great space if it's hidden behind piles of clutter. Choosing colors for walls and woodwork is a very personal thing, but you can create all sorts of visual effects simply with paint. Deciding on flooring, window treatments, types of furniture, and all those extra touches that make a house into a home are all essential.

THE LIGHTS

Where lighting is concerned, the more the better. This doesn't mean having a room that is over-bright, but one where light comes from many different sources, creating layers of overlapping pools. This gives a space both atmosphere and character, and can make even the blandest room seem interesting and welcoming. Make sure you equip yourself with an array of lamps, light fittings, and pendant shades, and let the light from each one illuminate the different areas of the room (see opposite, top left).

If you only do one thing

Set a variety of lamps about the rooms to give a soft light in the evening. The light from them will hide a multitude of unfinished features until you can afford to decorate.

Be safe! Never try to change any light fitting that requires rewiring yourself—always ask a qualified electrician to do the work for you.

Enhancing natural light

Not every room in your house or apartment will have the ideal amounts of daylight, so look at ways that you can enhance the amount of natural light that comes in.

• A white ceiling will act as a huge reflector, and pale walls will make any room look bigger and more spacious.

• If you are able to undertake some building work, fitting a skylight (see above left), adding an extra window, or putting glazed panels into doors can make all the difference and let more daylight into dark rooms.

• Don't underestimate the effect a good mirror can have. Placed opposite a window, a large mirror will double the amount of daylight in a room.

• Try arranging a group of vintage mirrors together too, for a sparkling effect (see left).

• Use reflective surfaces—a glossy floor, a piece of mirrored or silvered furniture (see above), sparkling silvery candlesticks—all these will catch the light by day.

• A glass or crystal chandelier suspended from the ceiling will sparkle in sunlight by day and twinkle at night too.

Ambient light

Your new home may not have more than light bulbs dangling from the center of the ceilings when you first move in, making every room look unwelcoming. Cover the bare bulbs with simple shades at first and invest in an array of table and floor lamps to vary the light sources and provide overlapping pools of light that will give instant atmosphere. Look for old glass shades in antique shops, try simple coolie shapes that look unassuming in a bedroom, or go for cheap card or paper shades at first. As time goes on, you can keep your eye out for interesting light fittings to replace them. Antique brass chandeliers, a modern chrome fitting, or a modern aluminum pendant can be fitted as you can afford it.

Why not try?

Making use of central light fittings and asking an electrician to fit a longer cable to form a low light over a table. If the light is not in the place you want it, fix a hook in the ceiling and loop the cable so it hangs in the right place—it's a great way to illuminate a corner (see above left).

For starters For all-round lighting choose a new paper shade to cover a light bulb, and don't sniff at the best value of all— the ubiquitous Japanese paper shade that will diffuse light beautifully throughout the room.

When you can afford it Look for more sophisticated light fixtures that will need to be fitted by an electrician, such as chandeliers, rise and fall pendants (see above right), and contemporary glass fittings. Also ask an electrician to fit dimmer switches wherever possible, to give your lighting flexibility.

Task lights

While you always need soft, flexible lighting for background illumination, for specific tasks like working at your desk, reading in bed, or preparing and cooking food, look out for stronger lamps that can be angled just where you need the light most.

For reading in the living room Try a tall, floor mounted lamp placed near the sofa or your favorite armchair that will give you a soft pool of light above your head (see above).

For reading in bed A table lamp on the bedside table bright enough to see clearly by is all you need. Place one either side of your double bed, so they can be switched off independently and one of you can sleep while the other reads (see top right).

For working For your office desk (or even for working at the kitchen table), pick out a bright lamp with an adjustable arm, so you can focus light exactly where you need it (see center right).

For the kitchen A spotlight in the kitchen mounted on the wall will throw a beam of light just where it's most useful (see right).

Accent lights

Use accent spotlights in rooms where you want to highlight special features. This could be a favorite painting or a display of photos, a decorative molding round the top of the room, or a beamed ceiling. In hallways where there is often minimal space, use down lights to wash the walls and highlight the wall itself.

Accent, or feature lights, can be as sleek and fitted as a set of recessed down lighters in the ceiling, or as simple and quick to put up as a clip spot attached to a high shelf and angled to pick out a particularly pretty bit of cornice.

Atmospheric lighting

For atmosphere and romance, whether you are having friends round for supper or spending a quiet night in together, make a point of adding lashings of twinkling lights. Turn down the dimmers and switch off any lights that are too bright, just leaving soft pools of light in corners. Bring an air of quiet contemplation to your bathroom too, or make a glimmering addition to your bedroom.

Soft, flickering candle light is a brilliant way to relax and de-stress after a long day, especially if the candles are scented, and the delicacy of fairy lights is always wonderful. Used together, candles and fairy lights are festive and fabulous in summer and winter, both inside and out.

Candle light

Candles come in so many different shapes and sizes that you can arrange them in groups anywhere round the room. Stack a set of large white church candles in an empty fireplace and you'll have an instant glow, or use glass containers to make romantic indoor lanterns. Place tiny tea lights in ornamental glass jars or even a set of vintage china cups that lost their saucers years ago along a mantelpiece.

Candle tips

• Put candles in the fridge or icebox for a few hours before use and they will burn much more slowly.
• Never leave burning candles unattended.
• After you've blown them out, but after the wax has become solid, cut gently round the top of a large pillar candle and remove the excess wax that has built up round the edges. This will stop the wick drowning as it burns down.
• Make pretty votive holders for the table. Tape two pieces of tissue paper around clean jelly jars. The white paper will diffuse the light from a tea light popped inside. Or use a strip of pretty perforated paper (see above left).

Make it in minutes

Save excess wax from pillar candles and stubs by melting it in a clean, empty tin can set in a pan of boiling water. Pour into a clean container with a length of wick suspended from a chopstick or pencil placed across the top. Add a few drops of essential oil like lavender, tea tree, or grapefruit to scent the room as the candle burns.

There's nothing quite like the glow and shimmer of candles and fairy lights to give any room a romantic aura.

Fairy lights

Fairy lights are traditionally used to light up the Christmas tree and they make a magical atmosphere twinkling away in the corner, but there are lots of ways to use fairy lights to provide sparkle and glimmer all year round.

• String a set of pretty flower lights along a simple shelf and see how they add color and decorative patterning to a plain white wall.
• Fix lights round a large mirror for a star-struck bedroom.
• Lights in the garden will turn a summer's evening into fairy land (use outdoor lights for this).
• Fill a glass vase with a rope of lights for a shimmering corner feature.
• Look out for LED low-energy fairy lights—more expensive but you'll be helping the environment.

THE STORAGE

There are different storage solutions for different spaces, and this can mean anything from buying new cupboards and putting up shelves to fixing clothes rails along a wall or investing in a proper built-in closet. Make it a priority when you move in or you'll find yourselves falling over boxes, bags, and assorted clutter.

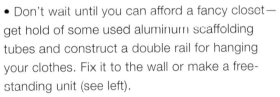

• Don't wait until you can afford a fancy closet—get hold of some used aluminum scaffolding tubes and construct a double rail for hanging your clothes. Fix it to the wall or make a free-standing unit (see left).

• Use card boxes to store all those things you don't need every day, like paperwork, sewing kits, photos, and stationery. Label them clearly and stack them on shelves to tuck them out of sight (see above).

• Put up narrow bookshelves for paperbacks in unlikely places, such as along a passageway or over a door, to make the most of all your space.

• Any spare bit of wall can be used for shelves, so look for second-hand shelf units and paint them to match the wall (see top right).

• A glass-fronted cabinet can look great if you paint it inside with a contrast color and use it to display a mix 'n' match china collection. It will keep china dust-free too.

Give yourself plenty of storage for all those things that clutter up corners and you'll be much more inclined to put them away.

Clutter busters

You'll find you will be much happier living with a bit of organization, and knowing where to find things when you want them is the best way to cut down on stress—you'll be able to think more clearly, too. If you have been living in separate places for some time, putting your lives together might mean that you need to have a good sort through your possessions and decide what you want to keep and what you can do without. You will be amazed by how much you don't need and how free it makes you feel to have a good clear out.

So get to grips with overflowing possessions and have a serious sort-out before you move in. Things can be organized into different piles that you can dispose of in some of the following ways, so stock up with black plastic sacks and get clearing.

- **Sell it**—through a nearly new clothes shop or on eBay.
- **Give it away**—to friends, family, or the local charity store.
- **Recycle it**—nothing is ever really "thrown away" so spare the landfill and find out where your nearest recycling center is.
- **Store it**—in closets, on shelves, in chests and baskets.
- **Display it**—put things in collections and make a neat display area where they can be seen at their best (see pages 62–7 for inspiration).

- *Messy bathroom bottles can be quickly hidden away in a lidded wicker basket (see far left).*

- *Tuck CDs, games, and extension cables neatly out of sight in a set of drawers (see left).*

- *Open shelves are a useful way to stack china where you can find it easily (see center left).*

- *Even a salvaged wire rack can be used as storage in a country bathroom (see below).*

Why not try?

Having a yard sale after you move in, even if you only have the tiniest back yard or garden? It's a great way to get rid of what you no longer need and to get to know your new neighbors, you'll have lots of fun, and make some useful extra cash at the same time. Print out some flyers advertising the event, post them through local doors, and invite all your friends to help you out on the day.

Built-in storage

Building your own storage is the most efficient way to use space, and this can be anything from a set of simple bookshelves in an alcove to a full-sized, floor-to-ceiling closet in the bedroom with interior shelves and hanging space that make it easy to tidy away clothes and shoes. From a custom-made cabinet in the bathroom, to a wall of built-in storage space in the kitchen or dining room to hold all your household china, towels, and even the ironing board and brooms, bigger cupboards are an investment well worth making as they will make sure you keep rooms clear and clutter-free.

Putting up shelves in an alcove

If money is tight and you are looking for a simple way of putting up shelves in an alcove, the easy bracket shelf is hard to beat. Used for bookshelves in a country-style living room, these simple alcove shelves are utilitarian but perfect for the job (see right). Use solid pine instead of medium density fiberboard, which can sag in the middle, and you'll have a set of shelves strong enough for the heaviest books or boxes.

1 Measure a length of batten to fit along each side of the alcove. Using a spirit level and rule, mark out equal spaces and draw a pencil line on the side walls to mark the position of the battens.
2 Drill two holes in each batten approximately ¾in (2cm) from each end.
3 Hold the drilled batten below the pencil line and make a pencil mark through each hole onto the wall. Drill a hole where marked and push in a rawlplug.
4 Use long screws to fix the battens in place.
5 Cut a length of solid pine for each shelf—measure each side as walls are not always straight. Place the shelf on top of the battens and paint to match the walls.

For starters For a quick and inexpensive storage solution, fix a cotton curtain across an alcove fitted with shelves, or in front of a shelf with a hanging rail underneath to make an instant storage space for just about anything.

When you can afford it Ask a carpenter to build you a cupboard in the same space, with useful storage inside. Instal pull-out drawers, wire racks on runners, hanging rails at different heights, and lots of different storage solutions that can fill every nook and cranny so not a single inch of valuable space is wasted.

Recycled storage

A set of tatty bookshelves found in a junk store or flea market, a battered chest bought in a garage sale, or an old-fashioned glass-fronted china cabinet that looks hopelessly out of date—all these can be restored, cleaned, and painted to make original and beautiful storage for every room of your new home. Whatever your decorating style, searching car boot sales or auction houses is an interesting way to spend a weekend, and will often yield fantastic bargains. Find furniture for free too, on freecycle, a global web-based community of people willing to give furniture (or anything else) away rather than take it to landfill.

Restoring and painting furniture

• Give any piece of old furniture a good wipe down using a dilution of detergent or vinegar in warm water.

• Rub it down with a fine-grade sandpaper.

• If it's bare wood you might like to stain it with a proprietary wood stain, then polish it with beeswax.

• If it's painted but battered (see above and far left), consider whether it might be more interesting to leave it as it is. A few knocks and scratches will give added character.

• If it's desperately in need of repainting (and this applies to varnished pieces too), rub it down well with fine sandpaper and give it a first coat of water-based undercoat/primer, then two coats of water-based acrylic eggshell (see left).

• For a "distressed" look, forget the primer, and use two different colors of water-based latex or emulsion paint, waxing edges and round handles between the coats with a candle. Rub down afterward with wire wool to expose the color underneath.

Unexpected storage places

There are always masses of places around the
house for sneaking in another shelf, a peg rail, a
box, or a basket. If you think creatively, you'll be
able to double your storage in out-of-the-way
places. Look at the spaces beside and over
doors—a set of narrow, painted shelves will hold
plenty of books when there's no more room on
the bookcase. You might find space along an
upstairs passageway wall, or over the sofa too.

A peg rail is brilliant for visitors to hang their
clothes when there's no room to put a closet,
and will also make a good place for individual
wash bags in the bathroom. Don't forget one of
the most useful and simple ideas—a hook on the
back of the bathroom or bedroom door to hold
a bathrobe or a laundry bag out of the way.

Extra places to store things:

• Baskets, baskets, baskets—in the kitchen, the bathroom, the living room—will hold absolutely anything and everything.

• Keep shoes in a log basket (see top right)—far better than having them scattered around the home, and it will be easier to find a matching pair when you are in a hurry.

• If you don't have a linen cupboard, roll up clean towels and store them in a wire basket in the bathroom (see center right).

• Put extra china on a high shelf round the top of the kitchen wall, or fit a narrow shelf below wall cabinets (see bottom right).

• Keep spare clothes and accessories in boxes on top of a bedroom closet and keep your bedroom clutter-free (see above).

• Have the washing machine plumbed in under the stairs.

• A cheap-and-cheerful stripy nylon bag will hold cleaning products or toiletries on the bathroom floor.

• Put smart storage baskets underneath a low shelf (see left), or on the bottom shelf in an alcove.

HOW TO DECORATE

Decorating is a big investment in time and money, so it's well worth preparing surfaces properly for a good finish that will last. There are lots of different types of paint, all with their own particular uses, but the main difference is between oil-based and water-based paints. Oil-based paints can be high in VOCs (volatile organic compounds) that can cause allergic reactions, so they must be used in a well-ventilated room to avoid headaches and sore throats. However, oil-based paint is tough and scuff resistant when it's dry. Water-based paints are quick to dry, brushes can be cleaned in cold water, and are generally less messy to use. Check out eco-friendly paints that have been specially developed to make a minimum impact on the environment—more expensive, but better for the planet.

Renting?

If you want to re-decorate, clear it with the landlord first before you put brush to wall. They might be OK about some color if you undertake to paint it back before you leave. They might even be happy for you to re-decorate throughout if the property is a little run down—but watch that they don't put the rent up when you've finished all your hard work!

What paint where?

Walls
- Water-based matt latex or emulsion
- Water-based silk latex or emulsion

Woodwork
- Water-based acrylic eggshell
- Oil-based acrylic eggshell
- Oil-based gloss

Ceilings
- Water-based matt latex or emulsion
- Water-based silk latex or emulsion

Floors
- Specialty floor paint
- Clear water-based varnish
- Clear polyurethane varnish

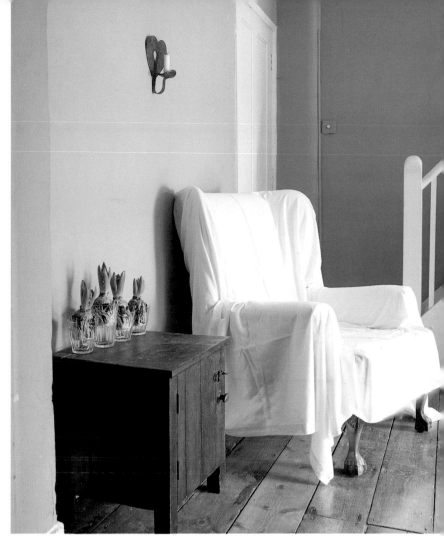

THE **WALLS**

Paint over wallpaper if it's in very good condition and if you are not sure what crumbling surface lies beneath. However, if wallpaper is peeling or bubbling, it will look amateurish and scruffy even when it's painted—it's much better to strip walls completely and fill any small pock marks with filler before sanding it down and then painting.

To prepare the walls

This sounds boring and is quite hard work, but well worth it for the clean, professional finish which will look great. Put the radio on and don a pair of overalls before you start, and you might even enjoy it.

1 Hire a steamer by the day and watch wallpaper peel off in satisfying shreds.
2 Wash down the walls with warm water and sugar soap to remove grease and old wallpaper paste.
3 Sand down with medium-grade sandpaper to remove any rough bits.
4 Apply one coat of cheap white latex or emulsion paint and you'll get a better idea where there are still lumps and bumps.
5 Do a spot more filling and sanding and then apply two coats of the main color for a flat, even finish.

Woodwork

Sand all pre-painted woodwork to provide a good "key" for painting, and wash it well with a solution of sugar soap and warm water. Give bare wood a quick sand and a coat of acrylic primer. Filling gaps along the tops of baseboards or skirting boards and around the edges of door and window frames will make all the difference to the final finish. A good tip is to gently brush over the filler with a wet paint brush before it dries. Leave to dry and sand with a fine grade sandpaper before applying two coats of top coat.

Wallpaper

Wallpaper can be expensive if it's good quality, but if used sparingly on a chimney breast or inside alcoves, it can look wonderful and make a room look very classy.

• If you want a funky, individual look, strip off the wallpaper and leave the resulting walls bare—great to live with while you decide how to decorate.
• Putting up wallpaper is best left to a professional decorator, which can be costly, but cut costs by having just one wall papered as a feature wall.
• For a much easier and cheaper option, paste posters, beautiful wrapping paper, or striking magazine pages directly onto the wall yourself.
• Hang striped wallpaper horizontally to make a narrow room appear wider.
• Paper the inside of a cupboard or closet door for a decorative treat every time you open it.
• For a budget piece of artwork, frame an off-cut of really special wallpaper in a clip frame.

All-white

If you are lucky, your new home will be painted throughout in a neutral shade, such as white or magnolia. If so, there's a wealth of possibilities for an all-white home—it's a wonderful blank canvas for you to put your own stamp on, and looks great with the clean lines of modern furniture or the prettier looks of country or vintage. If you need to re-decorate, you can't go wrong with white, and you can always add splashes of color with cushions, pillows, and throws.

But look at any paint shade card, and you'll notice that there are hundreds of different whites, from the cheap and cheerful brilliant white (marvelous in rooms that are flooded with warm yellow sunlight), to a multitude of soft whites with touches of pastels, and the more sophisticated "old" whites that are gray-toned and look best in older properties. Creamy whites, too, will look warm, and are especially good used in rooms that don't get a lot of daylight.

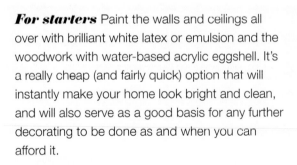

For starters Paint the walls and ceilings all over with brilliant white latex or emulsion and the woodwork with water-based acrylic eggshell. It's a really cheap (and fairly quick) option that will instantly make your home look bright and clean, and will also serve as a good basis for any further decorating to be done as and when you can afford it.

Ways with white

• In a room painted all white, add plenty of texture with rugs, throws, pillows, and cushions.
• White bathrooms and kitchens look less clinical with plenty of texture in the form of mosaic tiles or tongue-and-groove paneling.
• Add color with accessories like funky lamps, bright pillows, and a colorful rug or window shade, all of which allow a white room to change its character without the need to re-decorate.

*Paint a lobby or hallway a darker shade than
the room it leads into—the larger room will
look much bigger by contrast.*

Using color

Color is one of the best ways to give a home your own stamp, but it's not always easy to know which to choose. One of the biggest mistakes you can make is to pick a color from the tiny shade cards on display at paint stores without trying them out at home first. It sounds a drag, but it will save you spending valuable time and money only to find the color is too strong, or looks very different from what you expected. Bear in mind that all colors vary enormously depending upon the light (natural and artificial) that falls on them and will look very different on the wall to how they appear on the shade card. Pick out two or three similar shades and try out sample pots at home before you commit yourselves. Paint up large squares of card or lining wallpaper and attach them all round the room to see the different effects of light as it changes during the day.

Color know-how

• Go for a shade or two lighter than you think—color always looks darker when it's on the wall than on the shade card, and color looks different when viewed in artificial light as opposed to natural daylight.

• Make sure wall colors are the same depth and tone in every room to give the house a feeling of continuity and calm as you walk through.

• If you're nervous about using color in too many places, leave walls plain white and paint all the woodwork in a soft pastel color instead.

• Layer up color by using three different tones of the same shade on walls and woodwork and to pick out a feature like a fireplace or alcoves.

• Try creating the illusion of a dado rail by painting below a line drawn all round the wall, one-third or halfway up from the floor (see below).

If you fall in love with a bright, deep, or dark color, go carefully— use it in small amounts, say on a chimney breast, in alcoves, or on a feature wall, to avoid overpowering the room.

Color ideas

Color has a very strong effect on us, emotionally and physically, and the shades you pick will affect you every day, so it's important to keep in mind the mood you are hoping to achieve. Soft pastels look harmonious and calming, while a shot of brilliant color can energize and uplift.

Neutral Sophisticated and relaxing, use a combination of shades for a relaxing room.
Yellow Cheerful and spring-like, yellow reminds us of sunshine and summer days.
Orange Orange is energetic and stimulating—a warm, luminous color that is good in kitchens.
Red Seductive and dangerous, use red with caution as an accent color or as a feature wall.
Pink Feminine and pretty, pink is non-threatening and romantic.
Blue Representing peace, tranquility, and stability, blue is good to use in bedrooms, but needs a degree of natural light if it's not to look cold.
Green Thought to be a healing color and will always appear calming and relaxing.
Purple Has overtones of spirituality and wisdom, and looks contemporary and creative.

Use color to play with proportions and make walls appear to come forward or recede, to bring down a too-high ceiling, or to lift one that is low.

Play with color

Color can be used to deceive the eye and play all kinds of visual tricks, so use color on walls and ceilings to apparently change the proportions of a room. Pale blues, greens, and lavenders—all colors of the horizon—are receding hues and will give the impression that a small room is much bigger than it really is.

A ceiling painted in a strong shade, or a large circle of color painted on a wall (see left), can focus the eye and bring down the visual height of a too-tall room.

A long, narrow room can be made to look squarer if the far wall is painted in a warm earthy color like terracotta or red, both shades that appear to come forward. And horizontal stripes, both broad and narrow, will give a feeling of width, so use these anywhere you want to make a narrow space appear wider.

Color matches

Using soft color can be the making of a plain, uninteresting room. For a subtle effect, try picking two shades that are related. A pale warm green on the walls combined with a soft blue-green used on the front of storage cupboards will look interesting and unique, especially if teamed with plenty of white on the ceiling and woodwork (see right).

For starters Paint walls and ceiling with white latex or emulsion and the woodwork with water-based acrylic eggshell. It's a cheap option that makes your home look bright and clean, and will serve as a basis for future decorating.

When you can afford it Choose more expensive paint colors at your leisure, when you have had time to work out what you really want in terms of style and design. You may have a better idea of how the light works in the room too, such as whether it's light in the morning or the afternoon, and you can plan your colorscheme accordingly.

THE FLOORS

When you first move in, especially if you are renting, you'll be lucky if you have floor coverings that you like, are clean, and in good condition. It's more likely that you will have floor coverings that are completely unsuitable for your new, cool space and you'll no doubt want to do something about them, but this can be a very expensive area to change if you have wood or carpets in mind. Don't worry, there are plenty of budget options that you can choose and live with while you save up for something better—or you might find you like them so much you decide to keep them!

Thrifty floors

Sanded floorboards
If you have old pine floorboards, sanding them back to the bare wood and sealing them is a great way to get a hard-wearing, practical floor that won't show the dirt. If you decide to do the job yourself, be prepared for a messy, dusty time, but with such a great finish at a budget price it's well worth the effort.

How to sand a floor
1 Hire a sanding machine and edge sander by the day, and pick up plenty of sanding discs at the same time, both coarse and fine.
2 Kit yourselves out with protective goggles, face masks, and overalls—it's a dusty job! Pin sheets over doorways to adjoining rooms as the dust gets everywhere. Before you start sanding, knock in any protruding nails and screw in screws flat with the floor, otherwise they will tear the sanding discs.
3 Go over the floor once with coarse sanding discs, once with a finer one—and once more is perfect if you have time—paying attention to the edges and corners with the edge sander.
4 Vacuum the floor thoroughly before sealing with two or three coats of clear, water-based floor varnish. Alternatively, give the floor a white, bleached look by applying a thin coat of white latex or emulsion paint under the varnish.

Painted floors

Painting your old wooden floors is a much quicker job, and you won't have to sand too much. Just give them a quick whizz over with a fine sanding disc, or even sand by hand. Wash well with sugar soap and warm water for a clean, grease-free surface. Use a specialty floor paint, and apply two, or even three, coats. If you have concrete floors, do a similar job, but give the floor a very thorough vacuuming to remove dust before painting.

Top tip

If your home has brand new floorboards, they will be narrower and paler than old pine, but will be a perfect flat surface for painting.

Laminate floors

Laminate is one of the most popular budget floorings, with good reason. Made to look like real wood, laminate floors are available in pine, beech, ash, cherry, oak, or walnut effect, but are made from a thin plasticized veneer on top of fiberboard and plywood underlay strips. It's an inexpensive option, but take into account all the extras, such as underlay and edgings. You can fit it yourself, but get a good do-it-yourself book to help you. Laminate is great for laying over any type of floor as it clicks into place on top, with edging strips pinned to skirting boards or baseboards to hold it in place. Easy to maintain, laminate won't scratch and can be washed like a vinyl.

Tips for laying a laminate floor

• When measuring, add 10 percent extra.
• Store planks in your house for two days to let them acclimatize.
• Choose how you want planks to run—lay across the room to make it seem wider.
• Make any cuts on the back.

Vinyl floors

Vinyl is warm underfoot, easy to clean, and will reduce noise, especially if it's a cushion floor. Find it in sheets that come in different widths, or buy vinyl as tiles that are easier to fit. The latest vinyl floors are made to look like every type of flooring imaginable, from slate to sandstone, mosaic, wood, or marble. The cheaper brands look less convincing, but are a quick way to cover an unsightly floor. For the best finish, lay a hardboard base first, to flatten and even out the surface.

Tips for laying a vinyl floor

• Lay vinyl along the longest wall first. Ensure it's parallel by pulling away from the wall for 1in (2.5cm).
• Profile round a basin or WC, then lift vinyl and pierce above the floor. Drag the knife up, making triangular cuts around the base until it lies flat.
• Crease and cut off excess, then glue in place.

Rugs and runners

Wood-look, painted, or vinyl floors in living areas and bedrooms
are practical and cheap to instal, but they can feel less than
cozy. Rugs are a great way to soften the effect, or to cover up
a floor you don't like but can't yet afford to cover. They will add
color and texture and put your personal stamp on any room.
Look for cut-price rugs in the sales, scour flea markets for
beautiful old hand-made carpets, and pick up bargains in
local markets when on vacation. Stop rugs from slipping by
laying them on top of a piece of underlay of the same size.

If you can afford them, natural floorings give your home a luxurious look that's hard to beat.

Floors to save up for

Veneered wood

It's often difficult to tell the difference between a real wood floor and a veneered floor, yet there can be a huge difference in price. With a veneer, the top layer is made of real wood, as opposed to the plasticized image of a wood-effect, laminate floor. Built up of layers consisting of a pine base, a fiberboard core, and a thin veneer of real wood, veneered wood flooring is pretty stable and resistant to temperature fluctuations. It can be just as easy to lay as a laminate, but again, look at the price of underlay and adhesives needed.

Natural floor covering

Give your floors a contemporary, textured feel with any one of a range of natural floor coverings woven from sisal, sea grass, and coir. These floor coverings need to be fitted by a professional, which will add to the cost, but once down they look chic and are wonderfully hard-wearing if you look after them. It's a good idea to protect the surface with an environmentally friendly stain inhibitor, which can be done before it's delivered to you. When fitted, use castor chair mats to help prevent wear and tear, and blot up any spills as soon as they happen.

Carpet

The softest, most comfortable floor covering has to be real wool, or a wool mix carpet. Luxurious in your bedroom and cozy in the living room, wait until you can afford a really good-quality carpet, a cheap acrylic carpet is a false economy and will quickly look thin and grubby. For entrance halls, kitchens, and bathrooms, don't even think about carpet, for these areas you need something water resistant and washable and you are better off with laminate or vinyl. Pure wool shrugs off stains and is wonderfully forgiving, but a mixture of 80% wool and 20% man-made fiber provides a good balance of toughness and softness. In rooms where you want to relax and lounge about, carpet is hard to beat. If you move into a rented home where the carpet has to stay, consider having carpets professionally cleaned—it's surprising the difference this can make.

THE WINDOWS

Putting up curtains, drapes, window shades, or blinds is usually necessary for privacy in living areas, for warmth in winter, or to block out early morning light in bedrooms. But it's also the best way to carry through the design style you have chosen, so try to match the look of your window dressing to the rest of the room. Remember that simple, unfussy ideas always work best, and dressing your windows can be a brilliant way for you to get creative.

Keep it simple

There are lots of ways to make lovely window coverings without a lot of expense or fuss, whether you go for a simple pair of curtains clipped to a wire or an understated white roller shade.

Combining the two is one way to make window arrangements more flexible. Dress a pair of curtains to one side and leave them there as a decorative effect, just drawing down the shade at night. Tie a sheer curtain in the middle with a ribbon or make a panel shade for the lower half of a window for privacy. Get creative too, with unusual ideas that only need an eyelet punch to make a draped panel that can be hooked up in the day. There are hundreds of ways of finishing off your windows, so don't be bound by tradition.

Simple, unlined fabrics make the best window dressings for a first home. Easy to make and easy to put up, they will give you necessary privacy and filter light beautifully.

Curtains and drapes

They may be great for keeping out drafts in winter, but heavy lined and interlined drapes can be very costly. You might want to think about putting them on hold when you first move in, and use unlined, simple fabrics for curtains that you can make or buy ready-made. Try these simple ideas for quick-and-easy window coverings.

Gathered onto tape

A pretty curtain that will gather into soft folds can be made easily and looks especially pretty when made in a fine fabric (see top right). Simply hem all four sides, then stitch a length of curtain tape to the top of your fabric and gather it up on the tapes to fit the window; to finish, hang from the rings on the pole with curtain hooks.

Tie tops

Another speedy idea for easy curtains is to rip some strips off the edge of your fabric and hand-stitch them, folded double, along the top of the curtain (see center right). Use a set of ribbons or tapes stitched along the top edge or make a set of stitched ties. They can then be tied up in just a few minutes.

Eyelets

Eyelets are a brilliant no-sew option. Use an eyelet punch and make a set of eyelets along the top edge of your curtains that can be attached to a pole with a length of cord threaded over the pole and throughout the eyelets. Or, for a smarter look, use oversized eyelets and simply thread the curtain pole through the metal rings (see bottom right).

Tab tops

If you don't have time for sewing, or if it's just not your thing, ready-made tab-top curtains are easy to find in most chain stores and are quick and easy to put up. Just thread them onto the pole before it's finally fixed to the last bracket.

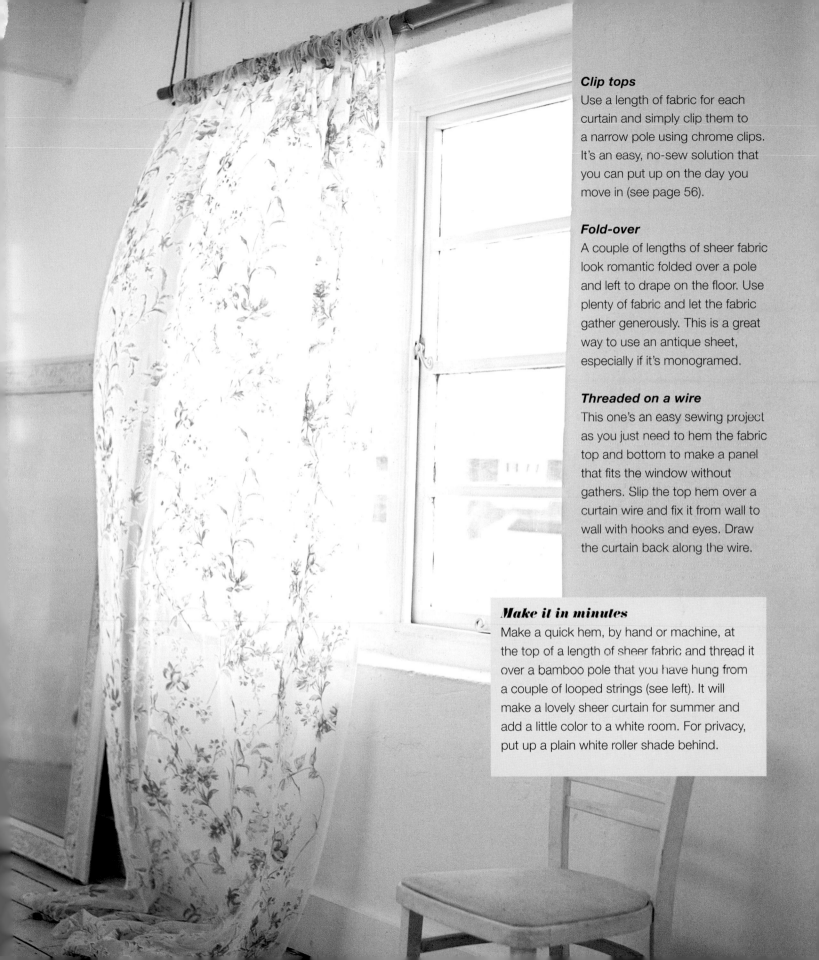

Clip tops

Use a length of fabric for each curtain and simply clip them to a narrow pole using chrome clips. It's an easy, no-sew solution that you can put up on the day you move in (see page 56).

Fold-over

A couple of lengths of sheer fabric look romantic folded over a pole and left to drape on the floor. Use plenty of fabric and let the fabric gather generously. This is a great way to use an antique sheet, especially if it's monogramed.

Threaded on a wire

This one's an easy sewing project as you just need to hem the fabric top and bottom to make a panel that fits the window without gathers. Slip the top hem over a curtain wire and fix it from wall to wall with hooks and eyes. Draw the curtain back along the wire.

Make it in minutes

Make a quick hem, by hand or machine, at the top of a length of sheer fabric and thread it over a bamboo pole that you have hung from a couple of looped strings (see left). It will make a lovely sheer curtain for summer and add a little color to a white room. For privacy, put up a plain white roller shade behind.

Blinds and shades

Window shades come in a range of designs to fit any room scheme, from slick, contemporary Venetian shades, available in metal or wood, to a classic Roman shade that looks smart and understated. Making a softly rolled Scandinavian shade doesn't require much sewing skill, and you can buy plain white roller shades from any chain store. As they don't need much fabric, shades are a wonderful way of using expensive, luxurious fabrics that might be far too costly to use for curtains. Depending on the size of your window, a yard or two of fabric is all you'll need, and you'll have a luxury look at a fraction of the price.

Venetian shade

If you're after a smart, contemporary look, Venetian shades (as seen here) are for you and are perfect in a home office or anywhere you need to control the light. The slats can be adjusted to open or close, and the whole shade can be pulled up and out of the way if needed. Venetian shades are also good for a window that looks directly onto a street, as with half-closed slats you can see out but no-one outside can see in.

Roman shade

This is the classic window shade, and one that is not difficult to make if it's unlined (see above). It's basically a rectangle of fabric that pulls up concertina-style, by means of a series of rings and cords. Find a book with easy step-by-step instructions and make it yourself. You'll save a fortune and have the huge satisfaction of having done it all yourself. A lined shade is more tricky, but not impossible if you take it slowly.

Roller shade

These can be bought ready-made in most do-it-yourself and chain stores, but go armed with measurements before you buy. The ubiquitous white roller shade will suit most rooms, and look almost invisible with the light coming through (see above right). Use on its own, or behind a pair of curtains. You will have instant privacy if you put them up on the day you move in, and curtains can come later when you've had time to think about what you want.

Scandinavian shade

This is a really pretty shade in classic Scandinavian-country style. Easy to make if you can follow some simple instructions. A wooden dowel rod threads through the bottom hem and rolls up and down under a looped cord (see page 57, center).

Make it in minutes

In the bathroom or kitchen, make an instant shade by cutting a new dish towel to fit the lower half of a window. Make a tiny hem at the top by hand or machine and thread it onto a wire stretched across the window and screwed into the windowframe. Great for privacy, but still lets in the daylight.

COLLECTIONS

It's true to say that pretty much anything will look like a collection if you gather enough of them together and display them unusually. If you love haunting thrift stores and charity shops, flea markets, and garage sales, you may have already picked up all sorts of interesting vintage china, glassware, old kitchen paraphernalia, and so on.

The danger is that you can become swamped under mounds of things that don't sit together comfortably and that you don't really use. It's much more interesting to start building a collection by limiting yourself to one or two types, whether that be 1960s rainbow-colored glass bud vases found at car boot sales, a set of pressed glass jugs spotted over months in thrift stores, or even by starting a collection of vividly colored cans from the supermarket. Choose something that grabs your attention or reveals your personality. Displayed with its fellows in their variety or similarity, the most ordinary thing can look interesting and quirky.

Ideas for collections

Here are a few ideas to get you started, but the list is endless, and all depends on what fires your interest. It's a wonderful way of expressing your personality and giving your home panache and individuality for not too much outlay.

- Glass bottles
- Tins, both old and new
- Vintage china
- Kitchen paraphernalia
- Jelly molds
- 1950s mirrors
- Glass or ceramic flower vases
- Tin toys
- Costume jewelry
- Paintings on a particular theme
- Colored glass

Give your home individuality and style when you make a collection of things that fire your imagination.

DISPLAY

Finding ways to display treasures imaginatively will greatly enhance your living spaces, whether you are displaying a set of photographs along a shelf or putting out your much-loved collection of vintage china on a dresser. Use your skills to create display areas especially for your assembly.

Paint an old glass-fronted cabinet to show off eclectic and colorful ephemera, pin diamanté brooches to a pillow cover, or fill a set of old teapots with herbs and flowers and arrange them along a window ledge—whatever your chosen approach the end result will be to create an individual ambience that reveals your inner creativity. Simply displaying framed pictures on the walls will give your home instant personality, especially if they are grouped together by theme, but make sure that they are not hung too high. Hang single frames so they are central to your eye level, and put groups together so that they can be viewed comfortably.

Hanging a group of pictures

Trace round each picture frame onto paper, cut out each paper shape, and fix temporarily to the wall with low-tack tape. Move them about until the arrangement works. Trace round each in pencil and hang each frame in its space. This will avoid making holes in walls where you don't want them.

Hanging plates

A set of old plates can look pretty on a wall and make a very economical way to inject character into a bland room. You can pick up vintage plates inexpensively in any charity shop, so look for simple color combinations like blue and white or pink and green. If you don't have a dresser, or wall-hung shelves (see left), attach wire plate-hangers to the back of each plate and hang in groups.

Still life

Try bringing together a disparate collection of objects and creating an eye-catching still-life display. A wire dressmaker's dummy picked up in a garage sale and strung with beads and fake flowers will make each element appear much more special because of its juxtaposition with the others. Or how about bringing out a few well-loved childhood possessions from storage—things you just can't bear to throw away—and displaying them together in a reminiscence corner? There are so many ways to show off quite ordinary objects, as well as your bargains and special treasures. It's just a matter of applying a little imagination.

Make it in minutes

• Find a few glass bottles, jam jars, or small vases, fill them with water and add just one or two flower heads to each (see below right). These can be simple country flowers you find on a walk, or a few pretty ones bought from the flower stall. Arrange them along a shelf or the top of a dresser, or simply line up a set of colored bottles (see left).

• If you have a decorative vintage dress that's too pretty to be hidden away in a cupboard, hang it on a coat hanger on the wall (see right). Lovely to look at, even if you never have the opportunity to wear it.

• Don't hide away your most gorgeous party shoes. Flaunt them on a display shelf and give them as much pride of place as a jug of exotic flowers (see below).

THE LIVING ROOM

The most important room in the house is your living room. It's the place where you want to relax in the evenings, chill out at weekends, and where you will entertain your friends and family. It's a room that will say the most about you, through your choice of color and furniture, through the cushions, pillows, and curtains you pick out, and through all the small pieces that you have collected and want to display around the room. You may be unable to change the kitchen or the bathroom, but there are a hundred ways of making your living room personal and individual. It's a multi-functional space that needs to be flexible enough to accommodate a whole lot.

WHAT'S YOUR FOCUS

Whatever plan you draw up, try not to put all the furniture around the edges of the room. A balanced room will always have a focal point—a spot that your eye immediately goes to when you come in and that all the furniture revolves around. In many homes this focus is the TV, but why not try to make yours fit in beside a more attractive central point?

Make a plan

If you drew a rough room plan when you first moved in (see page 10), now's the time to make use of it. Make paper cut-outs to scale of your existing furniture, or pieces you are thinking of buying, and move them around on the plan. This is a good time to try out lots of different permutations—can you fit in two sofas, or just one long couch and an armchair or two? Can you find space for a long storage unit or bookshelf? Where will you put the TV and audio equipment? This is your first home, so it's unlikely that you will be able to afford everything you want at first, so be willing to compromise and use second-hand furniture you may have been given, or found at a bargain price. You can still make the room stylish and comfortable, even if you are working on a budget.

A bookshelf or storage unit can make a brilliant focus if you have flat, plain walls with no features. Place it opposite the sofa and fill it with books, photographs, and collections of ephemera. Make it as tall as you can (floor to ceiling would be ideal), and you could even slot a flat-screen TV in amongst the books.

A special painting, print, or poster (see left) will make an eye-catching feature. A good place to find original pieces of art is at a local art school's end-of-term show. Or you might have an artist friend willing to loan you a canvas. If you're on a tight budget, frame a piece of interesting wrapping paper or hang a panel of fabric from a pole.

If you have a fireplace, it's the obvious place to make into the focus of the room (see right). A real fire will always look welcoming and cozy, but even if yours is out of use you can still make the space colorful and eye-catching with a display of logs or candles in winter and dried seedheads or flowers in summer.

A large mirror leaning against a wall (see above) is casual and understated, but makes a fabulous focal point while it reflects light into the rest of the room.

*Make your living room come alive with color—paint
all the walls or use it to add splashes of interest.*

USING COLOR

The use of color is one of the most powerful ways you can change your living room, but approach with care. The three main colors, or "primaries," are the ones we all recognize—red, yellow, and blue. Mixed together they become orange, green, and purple, the "secondary" colors. These are the colors that are the basis of all the others, and in their raw state are strong and vibrant and can easily overpower a room if used with a heavy hand—remember that a little goes a long way with any of the primary or secondary colors. But mix any color with plenty of white and it becomes a pastel tint; mix it with a touch of black, brown, or gray and it will be toned down to form a softer, muddier shade.

Luckily the paint manufacturers have done all the work for you, and if you visit any paint store you'll find colors that have been carefully organized into families to show off the entire spectrum, with tester pots that you can take home and try out. (See "Using Color," page 45.) An easy way to help you choose colors is to start with a much-loved painting, a piece of fabric, or a rug, and use the colors you see within it as the inspiration for the rest of the room.

If you are feeling a bit cautious about using color, there are lots of ways to bring it in without overdoing it, so why not use paint to add color:

• In alcoves
• Behind shelves
• As a feature wall
• Above white paneling
• On the woodwork only

Top tips
• If you aren't too confident using color but want to introduce some anyway, keeping the walls neutral or white, and introducing color in the soft furnishings is a fail-safe way to add as much as you like without fear of overdoing it.
• Look for a painting or print that has the colors you love (see above) and pick up some accessories in the same shades, or toning colors.

THE FURNITURE

If you are starting from scratch with no furniture at all, you may need to find ways to pick up bargains so you can furnish your living room without breaking the bank. There are lots of ways to do this if you're willing to be less than conventional and can look around for interesting alternatives. If you have a limited budget, invest it all on a well-made, comfortable sofa that will last you for years, and furnish the rest of the room with hand-me-downs or junk buys, replacing them as you can afford to. Or find other ways to make the most of what you can realistically afford.

Be creative

When you are on a tight budget, look for furniture designed for other purposes:

• A low, slatted garden table can work as a coffee table. Look at round metal garden tables too—they can look great next to a sofa or in a corner.

• A couple of inexpensive, flat-pack bedside drawers next to the sofa can be used for plants, photos, and lamps, as well as storage. Also look at storage boxes stacked on top of one another.

• Use battered old trunks for flowers and books, as well as somewhere to rest a coffee mug.

• Use a large basket to store magazines.

• Put a flat-pack coffee table under the TV and use the lower shelf for the DVD player.

• A couple of divan beds can serve as a corner sofa unit. Push them against the wall, cover with a throw, and pile loads of cushions and pillows on them. They will also be handy when friends stay over.

• If you can find one good-quality piece of furniture, like an antique wooden chair or a lovely side table, it will give a whole room of chain-store furniture a touch of class. Why not see if you know anyone who has furniture in storage and offer to look after something for them?

• Don't buy any furniture until you have taken the measurements home and tested them against your room plan or you might not be able to fit them in.

Living with hand-me-downs

When you first move in, you might be amazed at how much furniture will materialize out of thin air as friends and family offer to help and start looking round at things they don't need. In fact, the problem might be saying no! Be a bit careful here, or you might find yourselves landed with a jumble of furniture that you really don't like, so practice saying how grateful you are for the offer, but that it's not quite what you need at the moment. At the same time, don't say no before you've thought about it. With a bit of careful upgrading, painting, or covering up, you might be able to furnish your living room in an individual and interesting way for very little.

Bring personality to a plain cream room (see above) with hand-me-downs. Your parents may have given you a second-hand sofa, and your grandma might have donated an old closet that at first glance you might have been tempted to say "no thanks" to. But look again, and the closet can be brought up to date with a coat of paint and used in the living room as storage (see above),and the sofa's patterned fabric toned down against painted floorboards.

An old sofa can be easily disguised under a large cream throw (see above right). If the throw isn't big enough, a pair of tasseled blankets over the arms will cover every inch and a clutch of striped pillows piled up add color.

In lieu of a set of shelves, old wooden crates can be hung on the wall and make for informal and quirky storage. Even a battered old velvet chair can have its place and look stylish (see right). If it's a bit frayed, cover it with a sheepskin and throw on a couple of vintage-style cushions. Put it in a room with soft sheer drapes and a modern basket storage unit—the ancient fabric takes on a charm of its own.

Chain-store buys

If you like a stylish look that is modern and budget-priced, but don't fancy second-hand, head down to your local shopping mall. Many chain stores and DIY stores do a good range of inexpensive, well-designed furniture, much of it flat-pack, which cuts down transportation costs, leaving you to make up the furniture at home with (usually) easy-to-follow instructions. It's not furniture to last a lifetime, but it will help you to furnish your room at minimum cost.

Get the best deals by waiting until there is a sale at your local store, when they are selling off ends of lines, or find furniture that's slightly scuffed and offer the store a lower price.

Look for stores that specialize in furniture that's slightly damaged—it will not always be noticeable and you'll get a much reduced price. Or search out factory stores for bargains. Ebay sellers offer lots of new furniture at knock-down prices, and it's an easy way to shop from the comfort of home, but do check dimensions before you buy.

Avoid an all-embracing chain store look or you'll end up feeling you are living in the pages of a catalog—make the room your own by adding finishing touches:

• Frame an interesting piece of fabric or a series of postcards.

• Make an arrangement of decorative things on the top of a dresser or cabinet (see above), a set of baskets will double as extra storage, a vase of flowers, a clock, will all add interest.

• If you can sew, make a cover for a budget-priced wooden chair, or a set of pillows held in place with ties or add patterned pillows to a plain sofa (see above left).

• Put up contemporary box shelves and give the room extra color and texture by arranging vases, boxes, and books, but keep them tidy and don't let them be used for dumping clutter (see right).

• Look for an interesting light fitting and let it add the wow factor.

*Buy from the high street and put together a look that
is modern and fresh, but give it a twist of your own.*

Eclectic living rooms

Mixing styles, different ages of furniture, and decorative elements will give a living room a natural, relaxed look. Any room with this layered style will have a timeless feel, and one that seems to have evolved naturally, rather than put together in one hit. It can be all too easy to get all your new purchases home, only to find the effect bland and characterless. Use a combination of antiques, chain-store, hand-me-downs, and junk-shop buys for an eclectic mix that will let your own style shine through. Pull the look together by covering a chair or sofa in your own choice of fabric. If you can, see if you can afford just one good piece, such as a strikingly contemporary lamp, a worn but still beautiful Eastern rug, or an antique side table, to give the room a stylish lift. Compensate for buying a beautiful sculpture or painting that might have cost you a week's wages by using a garden chair with a cushion to soften it and a 1940s table as a desk (see above right).

Top tip

If you can, see if you can afford just one really good piece, such as a strikingly contemporary lamp, a worn but still beautiful Eastern rug, or a well-polished antique side table to give the room a stylish lift even if everything else is cheap and cheerful.

Mix and match furniture The traditional three-piece suite, with a sofa and pair of matching armchairs, can look dated. So why not try finding a selection of pieces—a hand-me-down or vintage leather sofa combined with a new one with a pretty flowery cover. This living room (see below) has been put together on a tight budget, with painted floorboards, a couple of mismatched sofas, and a small side table that doubles as a desk, but the floral theme has been echoed in the cushions.

A new and comfortable easy chair will make a wonderful centerpiece of a small living room but will be a long-term investment, so team it with a chain-store sofa and little else. Let storage be a pile of old trunks, and wait until you can afford it to build shelves or find a storage unit (see far left).

The minimal look

If you are very tidy and hate clutter, the minimal look could be the one for you. This style is usually associated with clean, contemporary furniture, and often comes with a high price tag. But the minimal look can also be achieved with a few carefully chosen pieces of vintage furniture in a simple white room with plenty of space around everything. The most important thing to remember is that each object will be very much on display, so every piece of furniture, vase, or lamp will need to stand alone and be worth looking at.

For a minimal living room

• Make sure you have plenty of storage and use it—the minimal look will lose its impact if it's not clean-cut.

• Keep on top of the cleaning, as every speck of fluff will be obvious in a minimal room.

• Let windows be dressed with the barest of coverings, like simple white or cream shades or blinds in plain fabrics that won't distract from clean lines.

• Lighting is key for this style, so look for well-designed lights that emphasize particular areas.

• Let ornaments be few and carefully chosen—this is the place for one or two really interesting pieces.

• Go for black and white, neutrals, or just a splash of a strong color like red.

• If you are furnishing your living room with the minimal look, whether that is achieved with contemporary or vintage furniture, make sure that whatever goes into the room is of good quality. This look just won't work with poor quality buys.

• A painting, a sculpture, or wall art will be seen at its best in the minimal room, so this is the place to invest in a really good piece, or make your own creative endeavor with natural materials (see left).

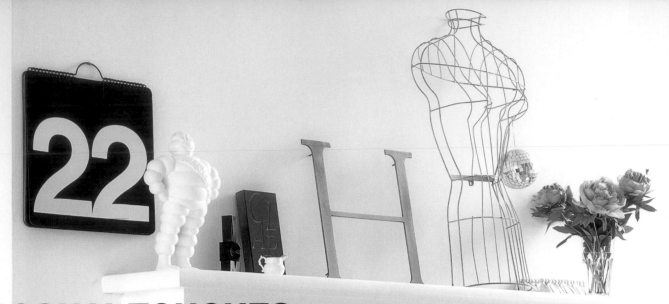

PERSONAL TOUCHES

Putting your own stamp on a room is often
a question of those small flourishes that only
you can provide. It's a very personal edge,
and one that will tell the world this is your
place and make you feel at home every time
you walk in. Weave your own story into
everything around you. The quirky clock you
found at the back of a dusty old junk shop
for a few cents on your first weekend away
together; a bowl of shells you picked up on
the beach on your honeymoon; a wreath
on the wall you bought for the first Christmas
you were married and liked so much you've
left it there, or an empty picture frame you
had for your birthday but haven't found a
photo for yet. Simply give your heart its head
and let your home echo your life.

Make it your own

- Display a series of framed black-and-white photographs of you both as children, stacked along a mantelpiece.
- Tuck a vase of pink Valentines roses into a bookshelf.
- Toss a patterned scarf you haven't worn for years over a white lamp shade.
- If you're handy with a needle, sew a clutch of pillow covers for the sofa using fabrics from old curtains.
- Make a cozy blanket for the arm of the sofa—if you haven't started knitting yet, this is your chance to learn to knit chunky squares in a simple stitch that can be joined together. Or knit some pillow or cushion covers to bring your own personality to the room.
- Flowers, flowers, flowers—and they don't have to be expensive. Try a pitcher of wildflowers brought home from a country walk and placed in the fireplace, a couple of blooms you picked in your back yard and displayed in a drinking glass, or a row of potted daffodils that you planted in the fall along the window ledge.
- Interesting stones can look like mini-sculptures, and if displayed on a mantelpiece or polished table top, they make a natural still-life.

THE KITCHEN-DINER

As life has become more informal and relaxed, the kitchen is more and more the heart of the home for most of us. If you have a kitchen table, you will find yourself using your kitchen for a lot more than just cooking—for eating, reading, working on your laptop, drinking coffee with friends, entertaining, and talking on the phone. So if you possibly can, make space for a table and chairs and give yourself a kitchen-diner you can live in. Your kitchen needs to be welcoming and relaxing, to express your lifestyle and interests, as well as being efficient and easy to keep clean. Your own personal style is just as important here as in the rest of your home, so knowing your look is the first place to start.

With wooden cupboards, floorboards, and chairs, this traditional country-style kitchen is given a modern edge with a coat of cream paint to bring everything together.

GET THE LOOK

No matter what your preference, here are a few design basics to help you choose a look.

Country Painted tongue-and-groove cupboards in white or blue and beech worktops keep this style warm and welcoming. Wooden chairs have checked or striped seat pads, and the floor is usually sanded or painted (see left).

Classic Modern without being clinical, a classic kitchen might have a painted dresser for contemporary ceramics, or cream Shaker-style units with wooden worktops. The table and chairs have a clean-cut style and the floor is ceramic tiles or vinyl flooring (see above left).

Contemporary Shiny surfaces and materials give the contemporary kitchen its edge. Splashbacks are often made from stainless steel or glass fitted above a shiny black granite counter or worktop. Glossy laminated units hide everything away except the high-tech coffee machine. Flooring is often dark wood-effect or slate tiles.

Retro Classic plywood chairs set the scene at a glass table in the retro kitchen, and retro-style appliances like a free-standing fridge-freezer and big toaster are key pieces. Walls are enlivened with a zingy poster or print, and counters or worktops are made from laminate or Formica (see above).

Vintage Old, unfitted cupboards and open shelving make a typical vintage kitchen, which is usually painted in soft white with faded floral fabrics and a zinc-topped table to accessorize. The sink is usually a reclaimed Belfast sink and the flooring is painted or stained boards.

GIVE IT A NEW LOOK

If you think you can't live with the kitchen you've inherited, think carefully before ripping it all out and starting again—you might have perfectly sound units hidden behind the scruffy doors. Replacing the cupboard doors will make an instant difference, and changing your worktops, sink, and splashback can make a dingy kitchen look new and save you a fortune. Look at what you can salvage and only replace what is absolutely necessary. A set of new faucets or taps can give a tired sink a new lease of life, but often it just takes a really good scrub with baking powder to revitalize a stainless steel or plastic sink (see page 153). Doors that are basically in good condition can be painted (see right). Wooden kitchen units can be bought up to date with a smart new color. Take up old, stained vinyl and replace it with a wood-look laminate or a new cushion floor. Sand up and seal the floorboards if they are old pine, or paint them.

• Wall cupboards can take up space and light, so removing them will make a small kitchen seem bigger and more airy. Remove only those that seem oppressive and put up a new set of wall shelves to replace the storage (see above right).
• A variety of different wall shelves and plate racks will give you an area for display and storage (see above left).
• Find replacement doors locally or on the web—choose flat doors for a retro or contemporary look, a simple Shaker design for a classic kitchen, or tongue-and-groove panels for a country or vintage scheme.
• Removing tiles can lead to problems, as you may find a crumbling wall behind. Use original tiles as a base and simply tile on top.
• Mosaic tiles are easy to fit as they often come on a backing of mesh. Just snip through the mesh to fit the required space.
• Create a random mosaic with broken tiles in different colors for a very personal style.
• If you are laying vinyl flooring, using vinyl tiles will make it much easier and you could design a patchwork or chequerboard effect.
• If you replace the counter or worktop it will affect the bottom edge of any tiles on the wall behind, so re-grout or fill the gap with sealant.

For starters

If you are renting, or can't afford to do major work just yet, you will be amazed at how much difference you can make with a coat of paint to freshen up the walls (see left). Kitchen walls quickly become greasy and stained, so wash them down with a sugar soap solution and give them a fresh coat of brilliant white paint, or choose a dramatic color to make a small kitchen interesting.

Painting the doors

Ideally remove doors from their hinges and lay them flat, but if you're worried about re-hanging, paint them in place, taking off the old knobs or handles first. Sand wooden doors thoroughly to remove old varnish or sealer and wipe carefully with a damp cloth to remove all dust. Apply a coat of primer/undercoat and leave it to dry before giving the doors two or three coats of acrylic eggshell or oil gloss. Sand lightly between each coat for a flat finish. For Melamine doors and for the side edges of cupboards, wash them well with sugar soap and warm water to remove grease, and undercoat with a specialty melamine primer or the paint won't adhere to the surface. Finish with two top coats, as before (see below left).

STARTING FROM SCRATCH

A new kitchen is expensive even if you choose a budget version, but it's the best way to pack in what you need, so plan with care. The cheapest option is to buy a flat-pack kitchen and instal it yourself, or get a local tradesman to fit it. If you pay for the fitting, it's possible to save money by doing some of the finishing yourselves. Most kitchen stores have their own designer, usually free. Make a list of everything you want before making an appointment with the designer who will draw a plan on their computer while you watch. You can suggest changes as you go and see a 3D visual at the end.

What you need from a kitchen:

• Enough counter or worktop space and work surfaces that are hygienic and hard-wearing.

• A good deep sink; a double or one-and-a-half sink is useful.

• Appliances: a stove, washing machine, and fridge are essential; add a microwave, dish-washer, freezer, and tumble-dryer if you have space and budget. (If you live in an apartment block, you may have communal washers and dryers so you won't need to factor these in.)

• Plenty of storage space for dry goods and vegetables, as well as china, cutlery, and pans.

• Spaces for garbage and recycling bins.

• Good lighting in work areas, both daylight and artificial light; flexible lighting over the table for a relaxing atmosphere at night (see page 94).

• Flooring that's easy to clean.

• A place to eat.

Top tip

If you're buying your kitchen from a do-it-yourself store a long way from home, you may be able to design the kitchen yourself using their online facility. But check via their website that they have everything in stock before you hire a van to bring it all home with you. It's a brilliantly cheap option, and very good quality, but the costs go up if you have to go back for a set of legs you've forgotten.

Space planning

If you have the luxury of being able to plan your kitchen-diner from the outset, it's useful to know about the classic kitchen designer's tool—"the work triangle." The three basic elements are the sink, the fridge, and the stove. When cooking you will be moving between these three areas, so make sure there's nothing in the way. You'll be draining boiling liquids into the sink and removing hot pans from the stove, so the kitchen is potentially pretty dangerous if you don't have a clear run.

Choosing a counter or worktop

Go for the best you can afford as it will set the tone for the whole kitchen. Here's quick guide to the various options:

Laminate Good value and can be made to look like natural materials, but needs protecting from heat and cuts.

Granite Will last a lifetime and look fabulous, but is expensive.

Composite Long lasting and very classy, but very expensive.

Solid wood Warm and comforting; scorch marks can be sanded out, but needs lots of oiling to make them waterproof. Don't use with an under-mounted sink or it will suffer water damage.

Ceramic tiles A budget option and can be used very creatively. White grout can discolor so use gray or natural; can also attract bacteria so needs to be kept very clean.

Choosing a sink

The sink you choose will depend on the style of your kitchen but the best are:

Stainless steel Easy to look after and hygienic, different price ranges and styles, but the cheaper ones are easily scratched.

Ceramic Looks great, and perfect for a country-style kitchen. Can get scratched if not protected and hard on fragile china (use a plastic mat in the bottom).

Composite Very hygienic and hard-wearing, but expensive.

Top tips

• When planning the new kitchen layout, make sure there's a worktop space next to the hob where you can easily put hot pans, and protect the surface with a trivet if it's made from laminate or wood.

• Think about fitting an eye-level oven, as it will save you bending to lift out heavy casseroles or pans.

Lighting

Good lighting is really necessary in the kitchen, so you'll need general lighting and more focused task lights, as well as a flexible way to light the dining area at night.

Budget option A track light with three or four spots can be fitted in place of a central pendant and the individual spots adjusted to throw light where you need it (see right).

More expensive Sleek and sophisticated, recessed halogen lights in the ceiling can be fitted exactly where you need a pool of light below; if you can't recess them, spots strung along a wire are a contemporary and stylish option.

Budget option Pendant lights over the dining table or a counter top will throw pools of light on the surface.

More expensive Flexible rise-and-fall lights over the table can be lowered for a relaxing light at supper time (see right).

Budget option Clip lights can be easily mounted on a high shelf and will throw light where you want it.

More expensive Under-mounted lights under wall cabinets throw good light on the worktops.

Top tips
- Have dimmer switches fitted to pendant lights for atmospheric lights.
- Candles are one of the most romantic ways of lighting a dining table.
- Use a qualified electrician to instal any electrical fittings.

Budget refit

If you have more space than money, you could think about starting from scratch, and make your own unfitted kitchen. Look out for vintage tables and storage units that you can place side by side. Fit a cupboard on a wall with shelves and a simple wooden worktop round a sink. Hide the space underneath with a curtain. If it's all white, the look is simple, unstructured, and charming.

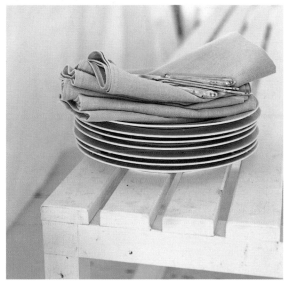

For starters Look for a cut-price garden table that fits your available space. These are often much cheaper to buy than conventional kitchen tables, and make a great starter set. If you don't want natural wood, paint it white or stain it any color of your choice.

When you can afford it Find a smarter table and chairs as and when you see them and when your budget allows. Find contemporary chairs at sale time, and look for a more substantial table at an auction house or on eBay.

Space-saving ideas

Many first-time homes have tiny kitchens that are much too small to accommodate everything you need, but a bit of creative thinking can often free up space you didn't know you had. So if you find yourself landed with a small, cramped kitchen with not enough room to eat and cook, don't despair.

- If you don't have space for a table you can entertain at, put a couple of stools under an area of worktop to use as a breakfast bar.
- If you only have room for a small table, use folding chairs that can be stored against the wall.
- It's not always possible to have the washing machine or tumble dryer in the kitchen if space is limited, so think about putting them in the bathroom if the plumbing can be fitted.
- Make a utility room in a closet in the bathroom. Put the washing machine and a drying rack behind doors, and fit a retractable ironing board that will fold away when not in use (see right).
- Use a rotating carousel unit in corner cabinets to store pans so you can access all of them.
- Use wall cupboards as base units along a narrow space, they are exactly the same height as standard base units but much shallower.
- If there's no room for a large fridge-freezer, think about having separate, under-the-counter ones. It's a more flexible option.
- Put a trash or recycling can under the sink where it can be hung on the back of the door.
- There's always wasted space on the floor under units, so investigate under-plinth drawers. Under-plinth heaters are also brilliant and give you the option to do without a radiator.
- A very narrow pull-out cupboard can be fitted into a tiny space and is useful for herbs and spices, or use the space for storing trays.
- Look out for racks and rails with butcher's hooks for hanging pans and utensils—these can go on a wall, or be suspended from the ceiling.

Why not try?

You may think your kitchen doesn't have room for a table, but if you think laterally you may find you can put up a wide shelf that hinges back to the wall when it's not being used. Pull up a couple of chairs and you have a place to eat and work (see right).

KITCHEN STORAGE

Tackle lack of worktop space in a small kitchen by maximizing storage so you can avoid cluttered surfaces. Without sufficient storage, you won't be able to clear up properly and work surfaces will become untidy. If you are renting and can't change the kitchen units, you'll have to make do with the space you have, but ask your landlord if you can put up a set of shelves, which is one of the easiest ways to create extra storage. If that's not possible, free-standing shelves can be a good alternative. If you own your house or apartment, you'll be able to do some DIY or have a professional build you some bespoke shelving, but look for ways to use walls, extra spaces on top of cupboards, and even the floor.

Extra storage ideas

• A set of wooden shelves on brackets is the simplest way to make extra storage for china. Fix cup hooks along the edge or underneath for cups and mugs.

• A built-in wall of open box shelving is a flexible way to fit storage and makes the most of every inch of space, but the finished effect depends on having china that looks good.

• More contemporary-looking is a set of open metal shelves. Fix them over the sink and you can use them as a drainer too.

• Do you have a space behind the sink? Use it for storage jars.

• Fit a high, narrow shelf all round the kitchen to display a set of favorite plates.

• Fit a shelf, or metal rail, underneath wall cupboards and above the counter or worktop for a bit of nifty extra storage (see left).

• Transfer dry goods like sugar, coffee, flour, and pasta into good-looking storage jars and keep them on a shelf to free up cupboard space.

• Things that are used less often, like covered dishes for entertaining, can be put up high to exploit extra storage on top of cupboards.

• Low-down storage is useful too; store baking pans that only see the light of day on special occasions at the back of cupboards, in tricky-to-get-at corner units, or in bottom drawers.

• Low shelves can be stacked with baskets and used for storing vegetables, pans, or dish towels (see right).

Top tips

• Open shelves look great and are a cheap way to provide more storage, but remember they will attract dust so you will have to clean them down every now and then and wash the china and jars—especially those not in regular use.

• A dresser or hutch is a traditional storage solution and is a useful buy if you are renting. A small free-standing unit will hold plenty of china and glasses and can go with you when you move.

• Stand a small cupboard on top of the worktop for glasses and tumblers; you can use the top as an extra shelf.

• A wire or chrome wall rack is easy to fit; store lots of kitchen odds and ends on hook-on attachments or on butcher's hooks (see left).

PERSONAL TOUCHES

Once you have the structure of your kitchen-diner in place, all it needs is for you to give it your personal stamp to add color and interest. A newly-finished room, especially a kitchen, can look bland and unlived in, but add quirky and unique finishing touches like these, and you'll know you've come home.

• Enamel storage jars from a bric-a-brac store (see below right).
• An antique set of scales—which you can use.
• Decorate wall space with vintage commemorative plates.
• Stand a painting on top of the dresser or hutch.
• Paint a set of old country-style chairs in different colors.
• Go for the "wow" factor and hang a flamboyant chandelier over the table (see left).
• Look for interesting vintage fabrics to use as tablecloths.
• Make tie-on pads for the chair seats using a gorgeous fabric (see center right).
• Add excitement to a white kitchen-diner with a medley of colorful dish towels, storage tins, ceramics, and a vibrant paper lampshade or bead curtain (see above).
• Frame a pop art poster.
• Hang a custom-made CD rack on the wall with space for the player beneath.
• Put up an oversized clock.
• Put up a painted vintage shelf unit and fill it with colorful glass and china (see top right).

ENTERTAINING

One of the delights of having your own home is being able to invite friends and family to share a meal with you. But don't forget that the main ingredient of hospitality is good company. No matter how simple the food or how small the space, any gathering will be a delight for both you and your guests if the atmosphere is relaxed and welcoming. Whether it's a late brunch or hearty Sunday lunch, afternoon tea or a casual evening supper, you can create a party atmosphere in minutes with a few simple flowers and tea lights popped in jam jars. There are times of celebration too, when you might want to dress up your table a bit more and use special china and glasses given to you as wedding presents.

Informal meals

Informal meals are a lovely way to see friends, but if your kitchen-diner is too small to host a large party sitting down, don't let lack of table space stop you. Set out food on the table or kitchen counter with piles of plates, napkins, and cutlery, and let guests help themselves and sit where they will. Put out cushions if you are short of chairs—most people will be quite happy sitting on the floor to chat and eat. Brunch or afternoon tea can be just as delightful as an evening supper, and a great way to entertain on a limited budget. Home-made museli, fruit smoothies, and muffins, or fried potatoes and eggs with lashings of hot coffee make a wonderful start to a Sunday morning; and what could be more welcoming on a wet Saturday afternoon than home-made cakes and a pot of tea? For evening suppers, it's just as satisfying to provide a bowl of hearty soup with bread and cheese, or a plate of pasta and salad, so don't let a lack of funds hold you back. You can always ask friends to bring a dish of their own and host a pot-luck supper.

A sit down spread

There may be ocasions when you want to host a more formal meal, and this can be a great opportunity to ask guests to sit round the table, so here are a few guidelines to get you started:

• Knives on the right, forks on the left, soup spoons (if you need them) on the far right. Dessertspoons and forks go across the top.
• Wine and water glasses at top right.
• Put down a charger, or large plate, at each place setting. The soup bowl goes on top and the dinner plate comes after.
• Napkins can go anywhere you like; on the side plates, on top of the soup or dinner plate, or placed on the right.
• Leave room for serving dishes and spoons.

Creative tables

Once you know the basics, there are a hundred ways of being creative and setting the table so it looks fun, original, or romantic. Sparkling glassware, simple flowers in glass jugs or jars, candles or tea lights, and a napkin for each guest are a good starting point. Lay a white cloth (or a pristine cotton sheet) or find a length of pretty gingham or striped cotton. Look for an old tablecloth in a flea market or jumble sale with hand embroidery, or use a length of your favorite fabric. A runner down the center of the table or across the width is an alternative to a cloth—make a simple one by cutting a length of linen to the right width and fray the edges. The setting can be led by the food, so if you're cooking an oriental stir-fry, use chopsticks and bamboo placemats; if making a pasta dish, give the table a bistro air with a red-and-white gingham cloth and napkins, and if you are cooking a traditional Thanksgiving or Christmas dinner, go for crisp white linen with a length of ivy draped down the center of the table and red candles.

Crisp napkins

Like a living room without cushions and flowers, a dinner table without napkins looks unfinished. Napkins are a great way to get creative, as well as being practical. You can get away with paper napkins everyday, but there is nothing to beat a set of real cotton or linen for that special meal. Let your napkins appear freshly laundered and pressed—it's a bit more work, but there's nothing like a crisply folded napkin to make guests feel pampered. Sets of real linen napkins can be expensive, but why not buy a length of fabric at sale time, or from the remnant box, and make your own? Make a set from brightly colored cottons and trim with contrasting braid or ribbon. Hem a few squares of snowy white linen or make a batch to match your colored plates. Wrap them with ribbon (see top left), braid, or a length of twine (see page 102).

Make it in minutes

• Roll up napkins and tie them loosely with a length of pure white pom pom braid for an elegant winter table (see left).

• A set of handmade napkins folded and tied with ribbon and wrapped inside tissue paper makes a wonderful gift and will cost very little if you use an inexpensive fabric (simply cut into large squares and hem neatly).

Candle magic

If you do nothing else to decorate your dining table for an evening party or meal, use plenty of candles to add instant atmosphere and charm. Pillar candles need to stand on holders but a china plate does just as well. Decorate around the base of the candle with flowers or a sprig of greenery (see below), or stand them inside a tall glass vase as a makeshift storm lantern and fill with sand, shells, pebbles, or flowers.

Tea lights look brilliant in all sorts of containers—washed tin cans, china tea cups, small glass votive jars (see left), egg cups, or drinking glasses decorated with a length of ribbon or a sheath of sheer fabric (see below left).

Make it in minutes
For a summer table display, place a pillar candle on a pretty cake stand and arrange shells or pebbles around the base (see left).

Top tips
• If the wick on a candle becomes too long and starts to get smoky, simply trim it with scissors.
• Always stand candles on a plate or in a holder to prevent them falling over, or hot wax dripping onto your table or cloth.
• Remove excess wax from votive holders by putting them in the freezer for fifteen minutes. The wax should pop out when pressed.
• Always make sure candles are fully extinguished when you leave the room. Also ensure that flames cannot reach anything flammable.

Simple flowers

Flowers always give your table an extra lift, but there's no need for expensive bouquets or formal table centers, even for special occasions. Your guests will appreciate a spray of apple blossom in the spring, two or three roses from the garden in the summer, or a pitcher of berries in fall or winter, but these are inexpensive and easy to find. Containers can be as beautiful as your favorite heirloom vase, a beautiful wedding gift you treasure, or as simple as a glass milk bottle, a special vintage pitcher, or even a teapot. Put a tiny bloom in a glass at everyone's place, or make a special arrangement of roses and a hand-written name tag for a birthday guest. Layer the look with a container of tall flowers in the center, and a couple of posies beside it, or set a row of single flowers along the center of the table.

Top tips
- Flowers look unassuming and simpler if you keep to blooms of one variety and color rather than mixing them.
- Put an asprin or a teaspoon of sugar in the water to make flowers last longer.
- If you only have a few flowers, use stems of greenery to fill up the vase.
- Snip off the ends of flowers as soon as you get home and put them in water. Snip ends each time you change water.
- Stop tulips wilting by pricking through the stem just under the head with a pin.

THE HALL and STAIRS

The entrance hall is the first impression visitors have of your home and your lifestyle, and it's also the area that greets you when you get home from work each night. Strictly speaking, the hall isn't a room at all—it's usually a corridor or passageway that you walk through to reach other rooms—so whether you pass through easily or struggle to push past coats and trip over shoes is going to make a big difference to the way you feel every time you enter or leave. The stairs need to be well lit so you can see where you are treading, but a soft pool of lamplight on a side table is one of the most homely sights in the evening. A mirror behind the lamp will double the amount of light at night, and in the day will reflect daylight into a dark space.

HALL STORAGE

It's all too easy to let the hall become a repository for clutter, so why not make it a daily resolution to put things away before they build up? One of the best ways to keep clutter to a minimum is to make sure you have enough storage, but building extra cupboards isn't always practical. Look for alternative places to put things away, like a space under the stairs where you can put up coat hooks and tuck in a shoe rack, or cupboards elsewhere in the house.

Put it away

If there's no room under the stairs, a peg rail on the wall will hold hats, coats, scarves, and bags if it's not overloaded. A narrow console table won't take up much room (see above), but a narrow shelf could be a good alternative if space is really tight. In a wider hallway, an upholstered bench seat or small sofa would be a great place to sit and pull on outside boots. You will need homes for: coats, outdoor shoes, boots, umbrellas, letters, keys, telephone, mirror, hats, gloves and scarves, and shopping bags.

Storage solutions

- Built-in cupboard
- Coat hooks or a peg rail under the stairs or on a long wall
- Shoe rack
- Umbrella rack
- Console table
- Radiator shelf or cover
- Bench with lift-up seat
- Small trunk
- Narrow shelves (either built-in or freestanding) for extra books and display
- Key cupboard

Top tips
• Fix a key cupboard to the wall in the hallway and slip your keys on a hook as soon as you come in. You'll save lots of frustration and wasted time looking for them before you go out.
• A radiator cover will immediately smarten up your hall and makes a slim shelf for holding keys and letters. It looks even better if you hang a mirror above it. You can order these as flat-packs online and have them delivered to make up yourself. Paint them to match the colorscheme of your hall.
• Build a small cupboard to hide unsightly gas and electricity meters.

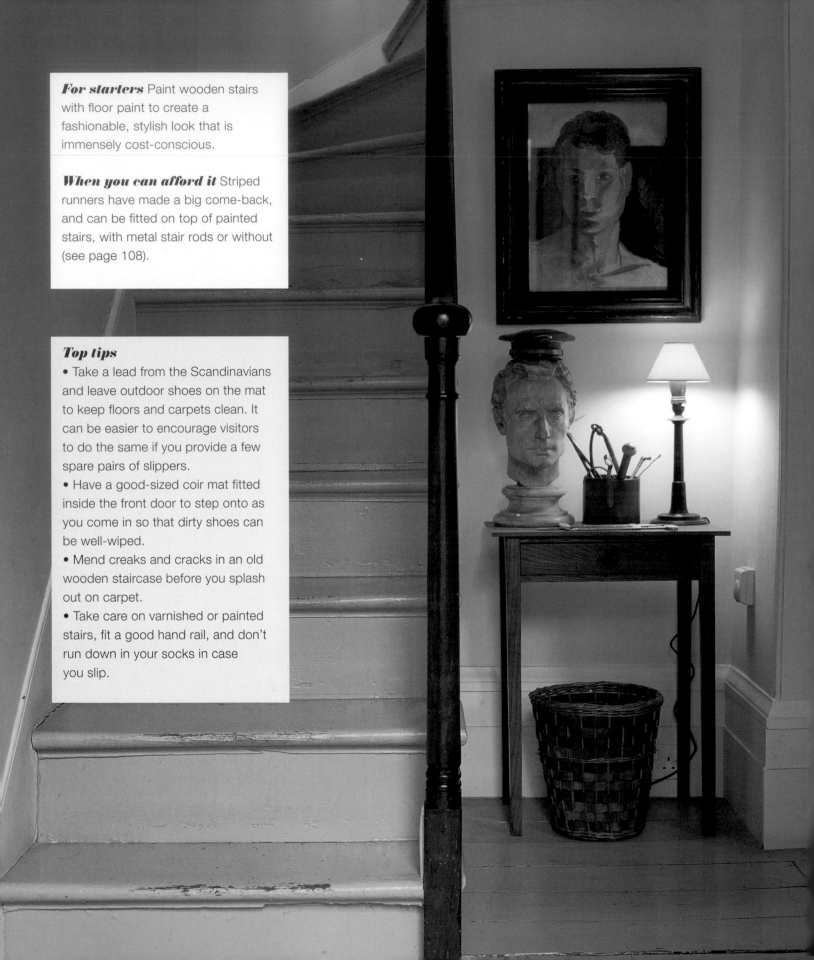

For starters Paint wooden stairs with floor paint to create a fashionable, stylish look that is immensely cost-conscious.

When you can afford it Striped runners have made a big come-back, and can be fitted on top of painted stairs, with metal stair rods or without (see page 108).

Top tips
• Take a lead from the Scandinavians and leave outdoor shoes on the mat to keep floors and carpets clean. It can be easier to encourage visitors to do the same if you provide a few spare pairs of slippers.
• Have a good-sized coir mat fitted inside the front door to step onto as you come in so that dirty shoes can be well-wiped.
• Mend creaks and cracks in an old wooden staircase before you splash out on carpet.
• Take care on varnished or painted stairs, fit a good hand rail, and don't run down in your socks in case you slip.

Look at vinyl if you want to emulate a natural surface—it's completely waterproof and can look like tiles, stone, slate, or wood. Carpets are rarely a good idea in an entrance as they get dirty very quickly, unless everyone is vigilant about taking their shoes off as they come in.

Flooring on the stairs

If you have chosen a washable surface in the hallway, it can be a comfortable contrast to carpet the stairs and to cut down noise from feet running up and down. Choose a good quality wool blend or the stairs will quickly become bald across the front of the treads. Natural floor coverings, like sea grass or coir, look clean and contemporary even in an older-style house and are surprisingly hard-wearing (see left). For a vintage look, strip wooden stairs and leave bare (see below).

FLOORING

With a lot of heavy traffic in the hall, a hard-wearing, easy-clean floor is the most practical option. The hardest wearing is a tiled floor like slate or limestone, but this can look and feel cold without a long runner to soften it, as well as being an expensive choice. Engineered wood is warm underfoot and looks great, but watch out that water from dripping umbrellas or wet boots doesn't get between the planks and damage it—hard-wearing laminate flooring could be a better choice.

Hard floors

One of the most budget-conscious ways to deal with a hall floor is to sand and seal original floorboards if you have them (see page 50). If sanding is too messy and disruptive, a pale painted floor will give a glossy, reflective, and hard-wearing surface, and is certainly the quickest and cheapest alternative of them all. But don't forget to prepare the floor properly and to give at least three coats of a specialty floor paint as it's going to get a lot of wear.

USING COLOR

The hallway and stairs are central to your home and there are different ways to make the link seamless and give the house a feeling of unity, so take advantage of this and use color to link the upstairs and downstairs.

Color flow

The stairs will be seen from all floors, so finding a shade that blends with the scheme of the house will tie them together. Even if you have chosen a series of soft off-whites for the rest of the rooms, a single color through the central core can be surprisingly effective. As you are only passing through, the hall can be the place to use color in a bolder way than other rooms. When choosing materials, think about wear and tear, and choose paints that are designed to take a few knocks and are washable.

Colorful walls

Paint all the walls, or just one, in a color that lifts your spirits each time you go upstairs. The hall is often dark and without natural light, with more light as you go higher, so any color will seem darker at the bottom and lighter at the top.

Colorful woodwork

With neutral walls, a staircase can look interesting if the woodwork on the hand rail and banisters is painted a soft color. Blue, gray, or green are always calming choices and look perfect with white walls and a neutral stair carpet.

Painted stairs

Painting is a cheap and cheerful option. Paint risers and treads the same color to contrast with the walls, paint risers to match woodwork and treads a contrast shade, or strip and varnish treads, painting the risers only (see page 111).

Choosing carpet

If you have the budget for a stair carpet, bring in color with a conventional plain wool-mix carpet. Carpet can be fitted from wall to wall or as a runner if you ask your fitter to have it cut down and the edges bound (see below). The new flat-weave, wool runners are woven like fabric, and need specialized fitting, especially if you have stairs that turn a corner.

Top tip

A narrow runner looks fresh and modern, but do be aware that fluff and dust will gather on the painted edges and so it will need more frequent vacuuming than a wall-to-wall carpet.

Top tips

• Decorate the rest of the house before tackling the hall and stairs. You may need to bring furniture, materials, and equipment through which could damage paintwork and floors, so do this area last of all.

• If you usually do your own decorating, having the stairwell painted may be the time to call in the professionals. It's often necessary to use a system of ladders and boards to reach the highest points, and it's not easy to decorate high up with a paint tray in one hand and a roller in the other.

• When you are painting stairs, it's best to paint alternate treads on the first day and the others the next. This way you can still go up and down if you step on each unpainted stair as you go.

• If you have a cat, make a barrier at the bottom while paint is drying or you'll have paw prints all over the house!

• If painting the stairs, emulate a runner and paint a strip along one or both edges. If you have the patience, paint a striped "runner" in any combination of colors.

• Choose a hard-wearing paint for banisters and hand rails—acrylic latex or eggshell are low in toxins, but will withstand years of use.

THE BEDROOM

Your bedroom is your retreat from the world, your very own private refuge. It's the only room that isn't a public space and you can be self-indulgent and creative, with no compromising what you want for needs of others. Designing the bedroom in your first home together is an exciting and creative project, so it's up to you whether you create a contemporary minimal space, a romantic country bedroom, or an individual room designed around an old piece of vintage furniture. You might prefer a simple, classic style or a more flamboyant, ethnic-inspired bedroom, but whatever style you choose, there will be a few key ingredients that every bedroom needs if it's to work on different levels.

CHOOSING FURNITURE

Unless you have a separate dressing room, you'll probably find that the bedroom is needed for more than one use and it's easy to overcrowd a small room. Draw up a floor plan and work out where the bed will fit, whether you can fit in free-standing storage or built-in, and what size bedside tables you need. Decorate the bedroom before you tackle any other room, it will provide a refuge when all around you is undecorated chaos.

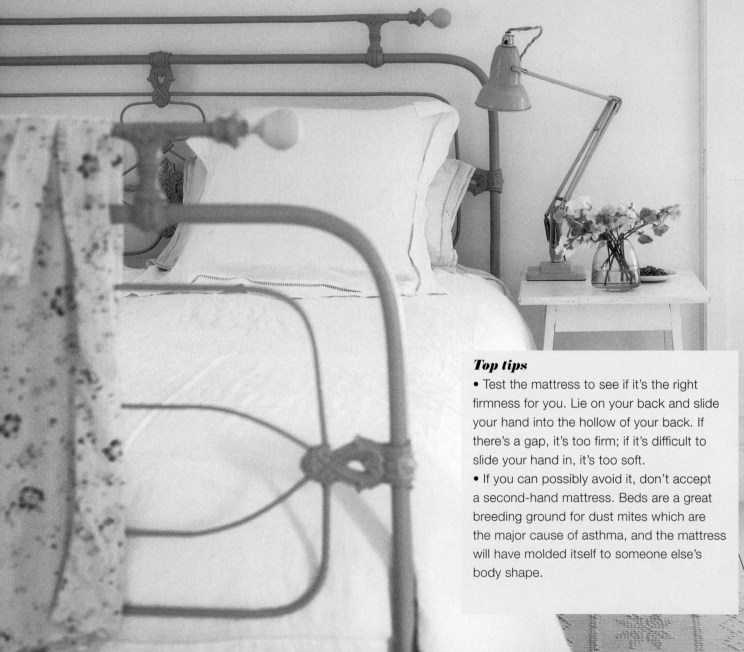

Top tips
• Test the mattress to see if it's the right firmness for you. Lie on your back and slide your hand into the hollow of your back. If there's a gap, it's too firm; if it's difficult to slide your hand in, it's too soft.
• If you can possibly avoid it, don't accept a second-hand mattress. Beds are a great breeding ground for dust mites which are the major cause of asthma, and the mattress will have molded itself to someone else's body shape.

The bed

On average we spend about one third of our lives sleeping. A proper night's sleep depends on a good bed, so if you only buy one thing for your new home, get yourself the best bed you can afford. Beds for two are available in different sizes, and generally the bigger, the better. You'll need to look at your budget and your own height and size as well as your room size to see which bed is right for you.

The style of your bed will be the starting point for the rest of the room, so go shopping knowing what style you want, whether it's a decorative metal frame, a solid wooden base, or a classic divan. As it will take up most of the floor space, the bed will be the biggest feature of the room with all other furniture fitting around it.

Try before you buy

Go shopping together and spend plenty of time lying on the bed in store. Don't be embarrassed—you are going to spend over 3,000 hours a year lying in bed, so take some time to get it right.

• You should both be able to lie down side by side with your hands behind your head without your elbows touching.
• Your bed should be 4–6in (10–15cm) longer than the tallest one of you.
• Bed sizes are not standardized, so don't buy a base and mattress separately without checking dimensions.
• A new mattress will age more quickly if it's on an old divan base.
• If you have an old wooden or iron bedstead, check that the base is firm and repair it before you add a new mattress.

Bedside tables

If you've spent your entire budget on a new bed, you can make big economies on the rest of the furniture. Bedside tables can be as simple as a pair of wooden chairs or stools (see below), a couple of storage boxes piled on top of each other, or a small chest of drawers. Build a low shelf either side of the bed for a clean, modern feel, or find a pair of tiny tables in a junk shop that you can paint to match the decor of your room (see left).

CREATING A FOCUS

Like the living room, your bedroom needs a visual focal point to give the room interest, but many bedrooms look disappointingly bland because of the lack of one. The head of the bed is a useful focal point. A tall, padded fabric headboard makes for a contemporary look, while a decorative iron or wooden bed head will give a more traditional style.

Alternative headboards

If you have a plain divan without a headboard, pile up pillows or give it a focus with a large painting or a set of small frames hung on the wall above. A beautiful piece of fabric hung from a pole behind the bed, a shelf for display, or a row of pegs with decorative bags can look interesting. Sometimes it can be tricky to find the right position for the bed, but don't rule out pushing it up to the window. The window itself can be the focus behind the head of the bed with a simple roller shade that can be pulled down for privacy.

Make it in minutes
• Add focus to a small white bedroom with a clutch of colorful pillows (see above).
• Attach strings across a wall and pin up a selection of black-and-white prints (see below left).

Top tips

• A feature wall of wallpaper makes an eye-catching focus behind a plain divan bed (as seen here).

• A small cupboard painted a striking color and dressed with a vintage mirror will create a pretty focus for a bedroom corner (see bottom left).

• Make a budget headboard with MDF: cut board the width of the bed, and 31½in (80cm) higher when standing on the floor. Lay wadding or batting across the front, take it to the back and staple in place. Stitch two widths of fabric together and staple in place over the batting. Stand against the wall and push the bed up to hold it in place.

LIGHTING

Lighting is one of the most important features in the bedroom. A variety of different light sources will make sure you can see clearly when you are dressing, give you pools of light for reading in bed, and make it easy to turn the lights down for atmosphere. Keep lighting flexible with a dimmer switch for the main light, and an extra lamp or lamp in the corner.

Daylight

Allow in as much daylight as possible, so try not to cover the windows with heavy drapes. Use tie-backs for lined or heavy drapes or make curtains from light, unlined fabrics (see pages 56–8). If you like a dark bedroom, a blackout roller shade will keep out early morning light until you are ready to face the day (see right).

Ambient light

A central pendant light will give you a general, even light. Look for light fittings that shade the light bulb, or choose a pendant with different points of light. A pretty chandelier will add a touch of romance. For vintage style, look in flea markets or on eBay for an unusual old fitting (see right).

Task light

For reading in bed you'll need a good lamp on each side so you can read or sleep independently. Stand these on bedside tables and either find a matching pair or go for a more eclectic look with two different lamps. You don't want the light to glare in your eyes but you will need a pool of light on your book, so make sure the bedside tables are high enough and that the lamps are shaded with a soft shade. Fit a dimmer socket to each lamp if you can so you can turn them down. For a dressing table, find a light that's high enough to

fall on your face while you do your hair and make-up—an anglepoise lamp has a flexible arm so you can direct light where you want it.

Romantic light

For an intimate, low-level light, it's hard to beat the glimmer of real candles. A couple of tall candles in the corner of the room will help create a relaxing mood and a few tea lights on a side table (see above) will give tiny areas of glowing light (remember to extinguish all candles before falling asleep). Experiment with fairy lights, rope lights, or a low-wattage bulb in a corner lamp.

For starters Find a pair of tall inexpensive chain-store lamps to put on bedside tables (see left).

When you can afford it Get an electrician to fit a contemporary light or two on the wall above the bed—especially useful if the angle of the light is adjustable (see above left).

STORAGE SOLUTIONS

Ideally you want your bedroom to be calm and relaxing to help you wind down and sleep well, so it's well worth keeping it free from clutter by having plenty of storage. Cutting down on hoarding is the best way forward, so don't forget the golden rule—if you haven't worn it for two years, get rid of it!

Free-standing storage

You have a wealth of choice, from second-hand chests of drawers to new modern closets. If you have a larger-than normal space you can pick up some great bargains here, as big wardrobes are usually difficult to sell. Old wooden furniture can be polished up to gleam with an aged patina, or rubbed down and painted, making it look smaller and less intrusive. Make a large storage unit from an old dressing table with its mirror removed and a smaller cupboard on top and paint it all to match. Customize an old piece of furniture with new handles and a coat of paint (see bottom right).

Built-in storage

Fitted closets can hide masses of possessions if the interior is designed to fit your space. Get a specialist company to design them, or ask a carpenter to build a basic carcase and fit it out yourselves with off-the-peg racks and shelves; the doors can be budget priced off-the-shelf louvers (see top right) or panels to cut costs. Flat, sliding fabric panels or a set of roller shades are a contemporary option and a couple of curtains on wires across the front will suit a country bedroom look. Low-level fitted cupboards can be designed to fit any space, a long narrow unit behind the bed is an efficient way to squeeze in extra storage, and alcoves can be fitted with shelves or hanging rails in a tiny bedroom.

Top tip
If you can't afford proper closets at first, look at canvas storage options, they are cheap and cheerful, but will get your clothes on a rail and behind a cover quickly and easily.

Shelving

Use a set of old or new free-standing bookshelves or build your own simple shelves on brackets in alcoves or under the eaves of an attic room to hold books (see left). Shelves are also a great place to display photographs and collections of ephemera, sets of storage boxes or baskets to hide away all those small things that lie about and cause clutter.

Storage boxes

Use storage boxes to make the most of all the under and over storage that you can—on top of the closet, on shelves, or inside fitted cupboards. If you have an old, high bed, there will be plenty of room underneath for keeping under-bed boxes and modern, roll-out boxes will fit under a divan (see above). Choose boxes and baskets that suit the style of your bedroom and do the job they are intended for.

Hidden storage

Make use of every bit of extra space by using furniture that has built-in storage inside but has other uses too, like a built-in window seat (with a lift-up seat), a blanket box, or an upholstered ottoman. These are really useful for extra bedding or for putting away summer clothes in winter. When buying a bed, look for one that has pull-out drawers in the divan which will give you extra bedroom storage.

COLOR

When designing your bedroom, color is one of the best ways to create a mood, whether it's relaxing and peaceful or more energizing. The calmest color schemes are those that are close in tone; choose a soft color for the walls and use lighter or darker tones for woodwork, ceiling, or trims. A favorite picture or a beautiful bed quilt can be good places to start, and choosing your fabrics first will provide a starting point. Pick out colors within the design to use on the walls and woodwork. Use color in other ways too, adding splashes of pattern and color to a room where walls and woodwork have been painted in white. Brilliant white can look stark, so choose off-white or creamy whites.

Create the style

You can say so much with color, so use shades that point to the look you want to create.

Country comfort Go for soft blue and white, or faded pinks with red (like this bedroom far left).

Contemporary elegance Use pure white alone or black and white with a bright accent.

Retro chic For a 50s look, choose violet, aqua, green, and blue, muted with hints of black; for the 60s zingy shades like red and lime (see right).

Vintage style Soft blue, old whites, and pinks epitomize vintage style (see left).

Classic look Choose a range of neutrals with white (see above right) for a pared-down scheme.

Oriental opulence Vivid sari shades with a mix of orange, hot pinks, and greens (see above).

Top tips

• Buy two sets of pure white bed linen so you can have one on the bed and one in the wash without taking away the main color interest.

• The atmosphere in your bedroom needs to be healthy and unpolluted, so look for paints with no VOC emissions (see page 38). Organic, water-based paints are the best option here.

PERSONAL TOUCHES

Make your bedroom into your own personal sanctuary with a few indulgent extras that will make sure it's intimate and inviting. This is the room where your senses can all be indulged, so introduce music, scents, soft textures, and flowers for a touch of luxury.

Top tips

• Launder real cotton bed linen before you use it to remove any finishing products.

• Give pillowslips and sheets a spritz of lavender water when you iron them.

• Air the bedroom every morning by opening the window for half an hour to let in fresh air.

Pamper your senses

• Put an oil burner on a side table or chest of drawers and use it with tea tree, rose geranium, or lavender oil for a soothing fragrance (see left).

• Make a sachet of spices to hang in the closet to give your clothes a delicious aroma, and deter moths at the same time. Mix cardamom pods, coriander seeds, and star anise in cheesecloth or muslin bags and tie to coat hangers or place them in drawers (see bottom left).

• Use soft textures, like a sheepskin rug beside the bed to step onto each morning, and a soft luxury throw across the end of the bed for extra warmth on a cold night (see left).

• Real cotton bed linen will help you get the best night's sleep, so look out for Egyptian cotton, it's the most luxurious and can be found at bargain prices if you look on the internet.

• Make a lavender pillow by filling a small linen case with dried lavender and putting it on your pillow where you can inhale the sleep-inducing scent at night.

• Put a radio or your ipod and speakers next to the bed for some gentle, soothing music.

• Keep a small jug or vase of flowers next to the bed purely for their beauty (see center left).

Make it in minutes

In spring, bring in a pot of hyacinths or scented narcissi to give your bedroom a delicate fragrance (see left); in summer the scent from a lavender wreath near the window will waft in with the breeze (see top left) and in fall and winter light a scented candle to transform the atmosphere in minutes.

THE BATHROOM

The ideal bathroom should be a warm, comfortable retreat where you can enjoy an invigorating shower in the morning or luxuriate in a warm bath at night. It's somewhere you'll love to linger, a place where you can relax and revive. But behind the creature comforts of plentiful hot water, underfloor heating, and heated towel rails lies a good deal of planning and design. Good bathroom design at its most luxurious can imply teaming sleek, contemporary fittings with a natural limestone bath and granite worktops, or it can represent a glamorous vintage look with a reclaimed, free-standing bath and a sofa in the corner. These are ideals, and not available to everyone, but with creativity and style, and by working cleverly within your budget, there's no reason why you can't create a bathroom you'll love.

GIVE IT A NEW LOOK

We would all love an efficient and stylish bathroom, but this isn't always within reach. However, it's perfectly possible to pare back to basics and add a few touches to transform a down-at-heel bathroom. A few clever makeover ideas will work wonders.

- For a budget solution, paint over tiles. Wash them down with sugar soap and warm water and paint them with a specialty tile primer. Give them two coats of an oil-based eggshell paint, covering the grout too.
- For a permanent cover-up, retile over the old tiles with mosaics and cover the bath panel, too—all-white tiles look subtly textured.
- A cheaper way to get the mosaic look is to insert a strip of mosaics into an expanse of basic white tiles—chip out a line of tiles first.
- If you have a white-tiled splashback behind the bath and basin, add a row of natural stone mosaics along the top edge for a contemporary look or add a colored ceramic trim.
- Dated, dripping faucets or taps really let a bathroom down so if you can, get in a plumber to replace them with smart new ones.
- If your shower has reduced to a trickle, replace the shower head for a luxurious gush of water.
- Replace built-in cabinet doors, or give them a coat of paint and replace the handles.
- Put up a new cabinet—one with a mirrored front will reflect light and look clean and modern.
- Replacing the floor will make a big difference. Prepare the surface with a sheet of hardboard first and fit a waterproof flooring like laminate wood-look or vinyl flooring. Don't use carpet as it will get damp and moldy.
- Sand wooden floorboards lightly and paint white or with a simple tile design.
- Give paintwork a good scrub and it will look so much better, or give walls and woodwork a fresh coat of paint. Use an oil-based eggshell or a specialty bathroom paint on the walls.

Color tips

• A pure white bathroom always looks fresh and clean, but add plenty of texture to stop it looking clinical and cold. Natural accessories like baskets, pale wood, and café au lait-colored towels add warmth (see above).

• If the white bathroom in your rented house is in good condition and you aren't allowed to change a thing, add color with colored towels, a painted cupboard, a retro chair, or anything that you can find to bring in your own touch—but beware of overdoing it and keep it simple.

• Add drama as well as color to a boring bathroom with fabulous wallpaper. Moisture-resistant wallpaper is available in most DIY chain stores and will bring instant glamor even if you can't change anything else.

• Bring in color by painting walls in a vivid shade and break away from bathroom blues (see top right).

For starters There's nothing more depressing than a grubby or moldy shower curtain hanging across the bath. Replace it inexpensively and in moments with a new one. There are lots of lovely colors available in homeware stores, but a plain white or transparent curtain will always look clean and fresh.

When you can afford it A plain glass shower panel won't cost the earth, but it will give your bathroom a smart new look quicker than anything else.

STARTING FROM SCRATCH

Apart from the kitchen, the bathroom is one project that you will need to hand over to the professionals, so before you order any sanitaryware, check with your builder that it is suitable and will fit the space. Showers can be tricky, as different showers are needed for various water pressures or hot water systems. There are many different skills needed to fit a bathroom, so try to find a professional who can do all of them, or someone who can bring in his own tried-and-trusted sub-contractors. It can be a good idea to let your builder order everything after you have chosen the style from the showroom or catalog as he will know exactly what extras are needed.

Everything you need from your bathroom:

• A shower, basin, and toilet are essential; include a bath if you have space. Put the shower over the bath, or have a separate cubicle if there's room.
• Plenty of storage for toiletries, towels, and cleaning products.
• Tiles or similar around the shower area and bath and behind the basin.
• A good extractor fan or a window for ventilation.
• A mirror and plenty of lighting (daylight and/or artificial), so design a lighting plan right at the beginning.
• Enough heating, including a heated towel rail.
• Waterproof flooring.

Small bathrooms

• Choose a wall-mounted basin or a range specially designed for small spaces if you have a tiny bathroom.

• A back-to-wall suite means you'll have no exposed pipework as it is all built into a panel behind the toilet and basin.

• Glass, chrome, mirrors, and a glossy floor will help bounce light into a tiny room, and a wall of mirror will double the perceived space.

• Keep it light—all-white will make a tiny bathroom look much bigger.

Wall coverings

The wall around a shower must be waterproofed, and tiling the entire area is the best option. Baths and basins need a small splashback to protect the wall behind from water damage, and where a shower is put over the bath, you'll need to tile the wall to the ceiling. In other situations, a classic solution is painted wooden paneling.

Standard tiles Plain white are the best value but can look clinical; get a new look by having them fitted in a brick wall pattern, called "offset," or fit rectangular, "metro" tiles (see left).

Mosaic Made in glass and ceramic as well as in natural stone, such as marble, they look terrific covering a whole wall (see top right), but it's cheaper to use them as trims only.

Stone tiles Real limestone tiles look contemporary and classy used as flooring and on the walls. They are expensive, but you can find look-alike ceramic tiles for less.

Tongue and groove Painted wooden boards fitted to the wall on battens give classic country style, but are unsuitable for shower areas where they will get water-damage (see top left).

Marine ply A brilliant budget solution, this is plywood developed for boat-making, so is flexible and waterproof. Use it for wall paneling or flooring and give it a few coats of varnish (see above right). Not waterproof enough for a shower.

Flooring

Any slip-resistant waterproof flooring will be suitable for the bathroom, and as in the kitchen, the material you choose will depend on the style you want. For a contemporary bathroom, choose natural stone, ceramic, mosiac, vinyl, or rubber tiles, or pick a wood-look laminate; painted floorboards, ceramic tiles, or natural look-alikes in vinyl are good choices for a vintage or country style.

Lighting

• Natural daylight is hard to beat, and if you can possibly afford it, have a roof light fitted into a sloping roof to bring daylight flooding in.

• You want privacy as well as light, so look at making a fabric panel that obscures the lower half of the window only, or fit a sheer white roller shade.

• You can spray the glass with a frosted effect or hang sheer cheesecloth or muslin—anything that lets in light while still giving you privacy.

• Make your bathroom light up with mirrors. A budget way to cover a wall in mirrors is to collect 1940s and 50s mirrors and hang them close together so they reflect natural light (see right)

• A wall of mirror glass will double the space and look spectacular in a contemporary scheme, but is an expensive option. Fit mirror tiles to a whole wall instead for a cleverly economical version.

• Fit a circular, glass bathroom light or a frosted globe to a central fitting. These will diffuse the light and stop the glare you can get from a light bulb and shade.

• Choose a couple of wall lights to sit above the basin, they will throw a good light for make-up and shaving (see right).

• How about a marine-style storm light from a marine chandler's? They supply individual and interesting waterproof mast head and bulk head fittings for ceilings and walls.

• Recessed downlighters in the ceiling are perfect for giving you a sharp, clean light just where you want it. If you have an indoor bathroom with no natural light, think about putting these In at some time, but make sure they have the right safety rating for bathrooms.

For starters The cheapest mirror light is a dual voltage shaver-light that combines a shaving point and a light, and a good first step when you are on a really tight budget. Ask an electrician to fit one for you.

BATHROOM STORAGE

Bathrooms are notoriously cluttered and difficult to clean. Jars, bottles, and beauty products all too often sit on every surface collecting dust, and moving them is almost enough to put you off cleaning. Sort out your storage and surfaces will be clear, and you will be able to wipe it all down more often.

For starters

As always with storage, you can be creative with chain-store and flea-market finds until you can afford a more expensive solution.

• Look for free-standing cupboards that you can paint. Fit them with extra shelves or pull-out wire racks you can buy for kitchen cabinets and use to store towels and toiletries.
• Fix a set of wooden shelves on brackets above the basin for inexpensive but stylish storage. Paint to match the wall (see above).
• Fix up a peg rail for towels and laundry bags.
• Put glass shelves across an alcove for toiletries.
• For a country bathroom, sit an aluminum bucket on a stool and fill it with soap, sponges, and face cloths.
• Find space in a larger bathroom for an old chest of drawers, and either polish it up or paint it. Use wooden trays or wire cutlery dividers from kitchen departments to categorize small things like nail varnish and manicure products in drawers.

If you can afford it, do it now

• If you are using a carpenter to line walls with tongue and groove, ask him to build out from the wall so that a couple of narrow storage cupboards can be inset into the paneling.
• Chop into the space between wall studs to make inset niches just deep enough for slim plastic bottles.
• Off-the-peg vanity units can be useful, with a built-in basin and storage underneath. These are often made from cheap materials, so look for one with frosted glass doors that will look more stylish, especially in a modern bathroom.

Worth saving up for

• Build an airing cupboard around the hot water tank, fit it with slatted wooden shelves, and you have all the storage you need for bed linen and towels. They'll get aired at the same time.
• If you have the space, a built-in shelf unit will neatly pack away everything you need to store in the bathroom, have one built across an alcove, in awkward angles in an attic bathroom, or as a low storage unit (see left).

PERSONAL TOUCHES

Whether you have been able to afford some of life's luxuries when designing your bathroom, or whether you have transformed a down-at-heel bathroom into a great space, there are plenty of ways you can continue to add a sense of comfort and well-being. White flowers are calming and restful, a shelf of clean, soft towels is inviting, and a clean, tidy space is one of the most relaxing things of all. Give your bathroom a personal touch too, with quirky finds from flea markets—a vintage wire soap dish, a "restroom" plaque, or an old wire storage rack.

Luxurious extras

• Display a few well-chosen bottles and sponges on a narrow ledge and don't overcrowd it. Keep away from a blue seaside theme, which can look out dated, by using neutrals and white.

• Tie a bunch of lavender flowers or mint leaves to the faucet or tap and let warm water flow over them to scent your bath water.

• Coordinate your toiletries and make a display instead of hiding them away (see right).

Top tips
• Invest in a set of soft fluffy towels with a matching bath mat to coordinate with the bathroom colors. It's the quickest way to bring a touch of comfort and luxury.
• If you are really tight for cash, dye a few graying white towels and a fluffy bath mat in the washing machine all the same color to make a matching set—it makes an amazing difference for very little cost.
• Towels will stack more easily if they are neatly folded; fold them into three lengthwise, and then in half and half again.
• Keep fittings and mirrors spotlessly clean (see pages 152–3) and your bathroom will always look at its best, even if it has to wait for a makeover.

Add a few finishing extras and bring a touch of luxury to your bathroom.

DUAL-PURPOSE ROOMS

In a small house or apartment every inch of space has to count, and doubling up rooms so they can serve two or more different purposes is the only option if you are to live life to the full. Finding a place for the computer is one of the first things you'll do when you move in, and whether you use it for social networking or working at home, playing games or writing a thesis, using your computer is a crucial part of everyday life. Inviting friends and family to stay and pursuing your own interests are important too, and it might seem that there's simply not room for everything. But don't let lack of space put you off, there's always a nifty way to make a sofa double up as a bed, to squeeze a computer console into a cupboard, or to make room for a creative hobby area.

THE WORKING HOME

Setting up home together means dealing with the household bills—boring but necessary. Even if most of your computer time is play or social networking, it's a good idea to have a set of files or boxes so you can keep records of paperwork easily accessible. If you use a laptop, you won't need much more than a corner of the kitchen table, but it's still useful to have a filing system tucked away somewhere. If you work from home, you will need much more storage to hold your office equipment and working files, but you don't want it to overflow and take over your home when you are trying to relax, so try to make a distinction between working and domestic time.

Top tips
• If you can avoid it, it's best not to have your office space in your bedroom. You won't be able to mentally switch off, and you need to be able to relax to sleep well.
• You'll need more electrical sockets than usual to accommodate the bank of computer, printer, and lamps required for working at home. Don't overload sockets with adaptors—ask an electrician to provide you with what you need.

- Customize a cupboard and fit it out with shelves and a metal workstation on wheels for a really useful computer station (see above). When you're working you can pull the whole thing forward, then push it away behind closed doors when you are finished.

- A working area in the corner of a room doesn't have to be utilitarian and clinical. A junk-shop desk with a couple of drawers and a shelf is more than adequate for paying monthly bills and will look part of the furniture, rather than an "officey" space that sticks out like a sore thumb (see left).

- Make a feature of a workspace. If it's an interestingly aged table and shelf unit, it will add to the character of your living room. Wooden divided shelves are easier to keep tidy and you can use some of the spaces for photographs for a more personal look.

- A second bedroom is the most likely situation for a home office. It's usually quiet and away from the living room, and you can close the door at the end of the day. Fit out an unused wall with a wide, long shelf with supporting legs to stop you feeling cramped. It will look sleek and feel spacious and is an inexpensive alternative to a desk (see above).

- The top of the stairs, or underneath them, is a neat place to build in a small office if the space is wide enough. Fit a worktop with a cupboard underneath for files, add a storage shelf for small office equipment and a really good desk lamp, and you have a compact home office that's neat and out of the way.

- An ergonomically-designed chair is important if you are working long hours, but they aren't always great to look at. So why not make a slipcover in a pretty fabric for a quick cover up?

- Kit yourself out with magazine files. A neatly stacked shelf will stop paperwork engulfing the room and look tidy if they are on show. See-through files will help you find what you need easily.

- Make an easy desk with two filing cabinets and a length of painted MDF balanced across the top. Find second-hand cabinets and spray-paint the lot for a low-cost solution.

CREATIVE SPACES

If you're working hard all week and don't have much time for yourself, finding time to use your creativity can be a great way to relax and de-stress at weekends. You don't need a lot of space for a small art table or a sewing machine which can be set out in minutes, but it's good to be able to leave it all out while you are working on a project. The kitchen table is in demand too frequently to allow you to be really creative, and there's more chance of enjoying your free time if you set up in the living room or a bedroom. A creative area can be a marvelous way of expressing yourself, not only in the projects you are working on, but in the colors, textures, and shapes of the materials and equipment you use.

Inspiring ideas

You don't have to have a great talent to make your own cards, sew a patchwork quilt, or knit a soft cushion cover. All these things underline the fact that home is where your heart is.

• A row of glass storage jars holding scissors, threads, and tape measure (see below left) make a pretty tabletop vignette.

• An antique trunk and a vintage file will disguise art materials and can be kept in a corner of any room (see right).

• A noticeboard of cuttings that inspire you makes an interesting display and will keep your creative juices flowing (see below right).

• A knitting project basket by the sofa with balls of soft wool that you can pick up and put down will bring creative life to your home.

• An old draper's cabinet with multiple drawers is a great place to store all sorts of creative materials where you can find them easily.

• A work table placed under a window will get the best light for sewing or other creative projects (see left).

• Keep materials and equipment in boxes covered in lovely fabrics (see below), or find other interesting boxes to store oddments.

MAKE ROOM FOR GUESTS

Having guests to stay is part of the enjoyment of having your own home, but if you are restricted space-wise and don't have a guest room you'll need to think about alternative places to put them up. Even if you do have spare room, it could well be used as your office and filled with papers and files. A single guest can be easy to accommodate on a sofa or day bed, but for couples a double bed is harder to fit in. A sofa bed is the best alternative so think about buying one when you are about to invest in a living-room sofa. Your spare room can do duty as both guest room and office, too, if you can fit in a sofa that converts into a bed. An inexpensive model will be less comfortable than a good one, but for the odd overnight stay it should be sufficiently cozy.

Fold it out, make it up, and pack it away afterward: there are lots of ways of making a temporary spare bed to put up guests.

• A modern divan or French-style day bed in the living room can be piled with cushions as a daytime sofa and made up into a single bed for a guest (see left).

• In an open-plan living room, make use of the space under the stairs to build an upholstered couch with storage underneath (see right). It will provide extra seating for when you have a lot of guests, and quickly turned into a single bed for a single sleepover.

• A built-in bed will take up less space than a full-sized divan in a tiny box room. Make a platform bed with battens and wooden slats along a wall or under the window and put a mattress on top.

• If you have a spare room, and space for a single bed only, consider buying a truckle bed; it's an extra single bed that pushes underneath the other.

• Buy a blow-up double mattress for occasional guests and put it down anywhere there is enough space—on the living room floor or in the spare room or office.

• Fit a wall bed and hide a fold-out mattress in a tiny space. Buy the frame and mechanism or the whole integrated system (see right).

• A double futon will fit into a space much smaller than a sofa bed, so is perfect if space is really tight in your office, spare room, or living room.

• Put up a peg rail with a set of wooden coat hangers so guests have somewhere to hang their clothes and you can use it for storing winter coats out of season.

WELCOMING GUESTS

A warm, generous welcome is worth any amount of
luxury food or a spotless house, so when friends or
family come to stay, whether it's for one night or
longer, make them feel at home with a few small
touches that show them you care about their
comfort. A spare bed in your office means you can
prepare the room before guests arrive, but if the
living room sofa is to be pulled out at bedtime, try
to have all the extras ready to hand so you can still
offer the same welcoming touches.

*If you do nothing else, put a
small jug of flowers in the
room—it's the most welcoming
touch of all.*

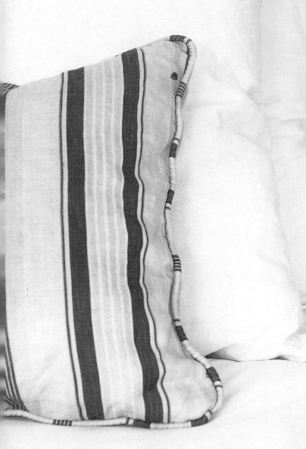

Make them feel special

• You may not be able to provide the most luxurious bed for your guests, but you can make up for it by giving them a plump set of pillows, crisp, clean bed linen, and a good duvet. Don't pull out your hand-me-down sheets—use the spare set of your best cotton, and have the bed made up ready when they arrive.

• Leave out a soft, fluffy towel and a new facecloth for each guest to use while they are with you. A small bar of beautifully scented soap will also be much appreciated.

• Make sure there is an extra-warm soft blanket on the bed in case of a cold night.

• Most people like to read in bed, so provide a good light that can be turned off without getting out of bed, even if you have to borrow a lamp from another room.

• With limited space in an overnight bag, a bathrobe is something we all usually leave at home. A cotton kimono-style robe will be very welcome for moving between the spare bed and the bathroom.

• Leave out a few really good novels and magazines for guests to read.

• You may not have a bedside table, but a low stool or dining chair will make a good makeshift alternative next to the bed for a lamp and clock.

• A mirror on the wall or propped on a shelf will be useful, and put a wastepaper basket in the corner too.

• A clock, a carafe of water, a tube of hand cream, a box of tissues, and samples of shampoo and shower gel are all little extras that will make your guests feel comfortable and at home.

• If the spare room also doubles up as your office or creative space, make guests feel more at ease by having a good tidy up before they arrive. Leave them a clear table top, an empty drawer if possible, and a place to hang their clothes, even if it's just a hook or clothes rail (don't forget to provide clothes hangers).

HOUSEHOLD TIPS

Don't stress about keeping house because you're too busy working to spend hours cleaning. There are lots of quick tips that will make your home look and smell wonderful, and make you feel a domestic goddess.

Make it smell like heaven

• For an instant spruce up, have a good tidy up and a quick dust, polish one piece of wooden furniture with beeswax and bring it up to a shine, plump up pillows, and add a vase of fresh flowers —the smell of beeswax will make visitors think you've been cleaning all day.

• Have a house that smells wonderful by cleaning hard floors with one of the bio-degradeable floor soaps. They are full of natural oils instead of harsh chemicals and will make your house smell like a home instead of a public toilet.

• Put a few coffee beans in the oven just before visitors arrive and the house will smell of welcoming fresh coffee.

• Put a cotton wool ball soaked in aromatherapy oil, like lavender or geranium, in the vacuum cleaner bag before you vacuum and the scent will fill the rooms.

Cleaning without tears

• Banish hard water marks in the shower before they happen; dry tiles and glass with an e–cloth after every use—they will dry spotlessly shiny. Try it on mirrors, too.

• To clean the microwave, cut a lemon in quarters, put in a heatproof jug and cover it with water. Put the microwave on high for 5 minutes and just wipe the oven dry with a paper towel.

• If you have let a saucepan boil dry and it's caked in black, burnt-on food, let it soak overnight in warm water and soda crystals and the black will simply rinse away.

• Remove scuff marks on vinyl flooring by rubbing them gently with the sole of a rubber trainer.

Everyday spills and marks

A glass of red wine on the carpet? Pour white wine immediately over it to neutralize the color and blot with a towel. Once you have most of the stain out, use a little carpet shampoo. Other red wine stain savers are salt and club soda.

Candle wax on the carpet or tablecloth? Rub with an ice cube to make the wax hard, then scrape off as much as you can. Place blotting paper over the wax and move a warm iron over it—the paper will absorb the wax. Repeat until no more grease appears.

Raspberry or redcurrant juice on the tablecloth? Dab the stain with lemon juice, rinse in warm water and wash in the usual way.

Ink stains on the sofa? Spray hairspray on the stain and dab it off—repeat, repeat, repeat.

Lily pollen staining furnishings yellow? Dab with sticky tape—the pollen will stick to the tape. *Do Not Rub!*

Love your cat but hate the hairs? Remove cat hairs from furniture by rubbing over with your hands inside a pair of wet rubber gloves.

Natural cleaners

Save money, damage to your eyes, skin, and airways—and the planet too—with household products that don't contain harmful chemicals.

Distilled white vinegar—a gentle anti-bacteria that will kill 99% of household germs, and safely removes limescale—dilute before you use. Use as a natural fabric conditioner, too, as it cuts through all powder deposits.

Lemon juice—will dissolve soap scum and hard water deposits and remove odors from cutting boards. Cut a lemon in half, sprinkle the surface with baking soda, and use to scrub dishes.

Baking soda—use it as a natural scrub instead of commercial abrasive cleaners; also use it to clean the fridge and remove any lingering smells.

Soda crystals—use these for cleaning just about anything from floors to kitchen cupboards, to unblocking sinks and washing down patios. It softens water in the washing machine and de-scales the pipes at the same time.

Top non-toxic cleaning tips

• Wash windows with warm water and vinegar, then polish with screwed up newspaper for streak-free glass.

• De-scale the kettle with vinegar. Leave it to stand overnight with a mix of half vinegar, half water to cover the element, and pour out the scale the next morning. Rinse the kettle well before using. Works brilliantly on shower heads too—immerse them in the solution overnight.

• Clean ceramic and vinyl tiles with soda crystals diluted in warm water—it will cut through grease in the bathroom and kitchen.

• For limescale in the toilet, push water out of the bowl with energetic use of the toilet brush, pour down vinegar and leave as long as you can.

• Polish your bathroom basin without scratching with baking powder.

RESOURCES

Gail Abbott is available for home styling consultations through Angel and Blume
www.angelandblume.com

DIY

Look up anything you need to know and how to do it on the following site:;
www.diyfixit.co.uk
www.houseprofessionals.com/diy

ONE-STOP FOR FURNITURE, BATHROOMS, KITCHENS, LIGHTING

UK
www.diy.com
www.ikea.com
www.homebase.co.uk

US
www.homedepot.com
www.ikea.com

KITCHEN/DINER

UK
www.theusedkitchencompany.com
www.neken.co.uk (tile panels)

RECLAIMED FURNITURE

UK
www.scavengers-uk.com
www.adpost.com/US.furniture/kitchen

US
www.adpost.com

FURNITURE AND ACCESSORIES

UK
www.next.co.uk
www.matalan.co.uk
www.cotswoldco.com
www.tkmaxx.com

US
www.mecoxgardens.com
www.comptoir-de-famille.com

LIGHTING

UK
www.davey-lighting.co.uk
www.tch.net
www.baileyshomeandgarden.com

US
www.historichousefitters.com
www.peddlersdesign.com

STORAGE

UK
www.theholdingcompany.co.uk
www.cotswoldco.com

US
www.containerstore.com
www.peddlersdesign.com

PAINTS
Organic paints
UK
www.earthbornpaints.co.uk
www.farrow-ball.com

US
www.farrow-ball.com

FLOORS

Worldwide
www.pergo.com
www.ikea.com

UK
www.diy.com
www.floors2go.co.uk

US
www.shawfloors.com
www.armstrong.com
www.homedepot.com

NATURAL FLOORING

UK
www.alternativeflooring.com

US
www.naturalrugs.org

WINDOWS
To make curtains and blinds
UK/US
So Simple Window Style by Gail Abbott and Cate Burren
www.angelandblume.com

Ready-made curtains and blinds
Worldwide
www.ikea.com

US
www.countrycurtains.com

FABRICS

UK
www.ianmankin.co.uk
www.vanessaarbuthnot.co.uk
www.homesandbargains.co.uk

US
www.vanessaarbuthnot.co.uk
www.fabricsusa.com

COLLECTING

www.ebay.com

TILES

UK
www.toppstiles.co.uk

US
www.daltile.com

BEDROOMS

www.sleepcouncil.com
www.bettersleep.org

Cotton sheets

UK
www.chilternmills.co.uk

US
www.smartbargains.com

Wall beds

UK
www.hideaway.co.uk
www.wallbed.co.uk

US
www.wallbedsusa.com

BATHROOMS

UK
www.ideal-standard.co.uk
www.bathstore.com
www.victoriaplumb.com

US
www.usa.hudsonreed.com

HOUSEHOLD HINTS

www.hints-n-tips.com
www.myhouseandgarden.com
www.eartheasy.com

FLEAMARKETS

US
www.findafloamarket.com
www.fleausa.com

INDEX

Photographic Credits

Key: a=above, b=below, r=right, l=left, c=center

Page **1** Debi Treloar/Helle Høgsbro Krag's home (www.cremedelacremealaedgar.dk); **2** Polly Wreford/Francesca Mills' house; **3** Christopher Drake/Nordic Style bedroom (www.nordicstyle.biz); **5** Polly Wreford/ Abigail Ahern's home (www.atelierabigailahern.com); **6** Polly Wreford/Foster House (www.beachstudios.co.uk); **8** Polly Wreford/Kathy Moskal's NY apartment, designed by Ken Foreman (www.kenforemandesign.com); **9** Mark Scott; **10** Henry Bourne; **11a** Winfried Heinze/Malin Iovino Design (iovino@btconnect.com); **11c** Chris Everard/New York apartment designed by Shamir Shah; **11b** Polly Wreford/Alex White; **12 background, a & b** Polly Wreford; **13** Polly Wreford/Mary Foley's house, Connecticut; **14** Chris Everard/Milan apartment designed by Tito Canella (www.canella-achilli.com); **15l** Polly Wreford/Foster House (www.beachstudios.co.uk); **15r** Jan Baldwin/Olivia Douglas & David Di Domenico's NY apartment, designed by CR Studio Architects (www.crstudio.com); **16l** Debi Treloar; **16r** Winfried Heinze/ Etienne Mery's home, Paris (johngo@club-internet.fr); **17** Polly Wreford/Kathy Moskal's NY apartment, designed by Ken Foreman (www.kenforemandesign.com); **18** Simon Brown; **20** Polly Wreford/Abigail Ahern's home (www.atelierabigailahern.com); **21al** Chris Tubbs/Emily Todhunter's holiday home (www.todhunterearle.com); **21bl** Polly Wreford; **21ar** Polly Wreford/Kathy Moskal's NY apartment, designed by Ken Foreman (www.kenforemandesign.com); **21br** Jan Baldwin; **22al** Winfried Heinze/designed by Sally Mackereth (www.wellsmackereth.com); **21bl** Polly Wreford/Foster House (www.beachstudios.co.uk); **22ar** Mark Scott; **23l** Debi Treloar/Susanne Rutzou's home (www.rutzou.com); **23ar** Andrew Wood/Guido Palau's house, London, designed by Azman Owens Architects (www.azmanarchitects.com); **23br** Jan Baldwin/Mark Smith's home (mark@smithcreative.net); **24al** Andrew Wood/Christer Wallensteen's apartment, Stockholm; **24ar** Jan Baldwin/Jan Hashey & Yasuo Minagawa; **24cr** Polly Wreford/Charlotte-Anne Fidler's home, London; **24br** Polly Wreford/Clare Nash; **25** Chris Everard/designed by Helen Ellery of The Plot London; **26l** Polly Wreford; **26r** Mark Scott; **27** Polly Wreford; **28** Debi Treloar/Mark & Sally Bailey's house (www.baileyshomeandgarden.com); **29l** Polly Wreford; **29r** Polly Wreford/Foster House (www.beachstudios.co.uk); **30l** Chris Everard; **30c** Winfried Heinze; **30-31 main** Debi Treloar/guesthouse of Philippe Guilmin, Brussels (philippe.guilmin@skynet.be); **31r** Henry Bourne; **32al** Winfried Heinze/designed by Henri Fitzwilliam-Lay (hfitz@hotmail.com); **32ar** Dan Duchars/stylist Rose Hammick, architect Andrew Treverton; **32b** Chris Everard/designed by Helen Ellery of The Plot London; **33 main** Mark Scott; **33 inset** Polly Wreford/Marie-Hélène de Taillac (www.mariehelenedetaillac.com); **34-35** Debi Treloar/Paul Balland & Jane Wadham of jwflowers.com, London; **35al** Mark Scott; **35bl** Polly Wreford/Tom Fallon's home, Shelter Island; **35r** Debi Treloar/ Helle Høgsbro Krag's home (www.cremedelacremealaedgar.dk); **36** Jan Baldwin/Claire Haithwaite & Dean Maryon, Amsterdam; **37l** Polly Wreford/Michael Bains & Catherine Woram's home (www.catherineworam.co.uk); **37ar** Winfried Heinze; **37cr** Polly Wreford/Foster House (www.beachstudios.co.uk); **37br** Polly Wreford/Sasha Waddell's home (www.beachstudios.co.uk/www.sashawaddelldesign.com); **38** Polly Wreford/Marie-Hélène de Taillac (www.mariehelenedetaillac.com); **39al** Winfried Heinze/www.baroquegarden.com; **39ar** Henry Bourne; **39br** Sus Rosenquist/Jette Riis & Lars Hansen's home, Denmark; **40** Debi Treloar/Sanne Hjermind & Claes Bech-Poulsen (www.claesbp.dk); **41** background Polly Wreford; **41al** Polly Wreford/Lois Draegin & David Cohen's home; **41br** Polly Wreford/Emma Greenhill (egreenhill@freenet.co.uk); **42** Polly Wreford/Sasha Waddell's home (www.beachstudios.co.uk/ www.sashawaddelldesign.com); **43al** Polly Wreford/ www.atlantabartlett.com; **43ar** Polly Wreford/Siobhán McKeating's home (www.brissi.co.uk); **43br** Simon Brown; **44** Tom Leighton; **45l** Henry Bourne; **45r** Winfried Heinze/Etienne Mery's home, Paris (johngo@club-internet.fr); **46a** Chris Everard/Yuen-Wei Chew's London apartment, designed by Paul Daly Design Studio Ltd (www.pauldaly.com); **46bl** Henry Bourne; **46 br** CICO; **47** Simon Brown; **48** Jan Baldwin/Claire Haithwaite & Dean Maryon, Amsterdam; **49** Tom Leighton/ www.farrow-ball.com; **50a** Polly Wreford/Clare Nash; **50b** Debi Treloar/Mark & Sally Bailey's house (www.baileyshomeandgarden.com); **51** Chris Everard/www.emmabridgewater.co.uk; **52a** Polly Wreford/Kathy Moskal's NY apartment, designed by Ken Foreman(www.kenforemandesign.com); **52b** Christopher Drake/ Maurizio Epifani's home, Milan (www.lorodeifarlocchi.com); **53** Simon Upton/Zara Colchester; **54l** Polly Wreford/ apartment of Amy Harte Hossfeld & Martin Hossfeld (www.2712design.com); **54r** Henry Bourne; **55** Debi Treloar/Clare & David Mannix-Andrews' house; **56** Mark Scott; **57l** Mark Scott; **57r** Mark Scott; **58a** Mark Scott; **58c** Debi Treloar/Sanne Hjermind & Claes Bech-Poulsen (www.claesbp.dk); **58b** Mark Scott; **59** Polly Wreford/ www.atlantabartlett.com; **60** Tom Leighton; **61al** Debi Treloar/Nicky Phillips' apartment; **61ar** Polly Wreford /Harriet Maxwell Macdonald's home (www.ochre.net); **61br** ph James Merrell; **62** Debi Treloar; **63l** Debi Treloar/guesthouse of Philippe Guilmin (philippe.guilmin@skynet.be); **63ar** Mark Scott; **63br** Winfried Heinze/ Stella's room in NYC; **64** Simon Brown; **65a** Debi Treloar/designer Susanne Rutzou's home (www.rutzou.com); **65b** Mark Scott; **66** Simon Brown; **67bl** Polly Wreford; **67ar** Polly Wreford/Emma Greenhill (egreenhill@freenet.co.uk); **67br** James Merrell; **68** Polly Wreford/ www.atlantabartlett.com; **70a** Polly Wreford/Clare Nash; **70b** Lina Ikse Bergman/ Jette Arendal Winther & Niels Winther's home, Denmark (www.arendal-ceramics.com); **71** Polly Wreford/Emma Greenhill (egreenhill@freenet.co.uk); **72** Polly Wreford /Louise Jackson's house; **73** Polly Wreford/Robert Merrett & Luis Peral's apartment (robert.merrett @macunlimited.net); **74-75** Christopher Drake/house designed by Angela A'Court (orangedawe@hotmail.com); **76** Debi Treloar/Patty Collister' home (www.anangelatmytable.com); **77al** Debi Treloar/Helle Høgsbro Krag's home (www.cremedelacremealaedgar.dk); **77a**r Debi Treloar/Mark & Sally Bailey's home (www. baileyshomeandgarden.com); **77br** Polly Wreford/Foster House (www.beachstudios.co.uk); **78l** Polly Wreford/ Mary Foley's house, Connecticut; **78r** CICO; **79** Debi Treloar/Nicky Phillips' apartment; **80l** Adria Ellis' apartment, New York; **80r** Sandra Lane/Paul Balland & Jane Wadham (jwflowers.com); **81** Polly Wreford/ www.atlantabartlett.com; **82** Polly Wreford/Laurent Bayard's home (020 7328 2022); **83al** Andrew Wood/ Michael Asplund's apartment, Stockholm (www.asplund.org); **83ar** Chris Everard/ Amy Harte Hossfeld & Martin Hossfeld's home (www.2712design.com); **83br** Jan Baldwin/Mona Nerenberg & Lisa Bynon's house (Bloom, Sag Harbor +1 631 725 4680); 84 Polly Wreford/Clare Nash; **85al** Polly Wreford/ www.atlantabartlett.com; **85ac** Sandra Lane; **85ar** Simon Brown; **85b** Debi Treloar/designed by architect Amanda Martocchio & Gustavo Martinez Design (www.gustavomartinezdesign.com); **86** Christopher Drake/house designed by Helen Ellery (www.theplotlondon.com); **88** Polly Wreford/Sasha Waddell's home (www.beachstudios.co.uk/ www.sashawaddelldesign.com); **89l** Christopher Drake/designed by Angela A'Court (orangedawe@hotmail.com); **89r** Andrew Wood/Jane Collins of Sixty 6, Marylebone High St, London; **90l** Chris Tubbs/Powers house, London (Judd Street Gallery); **90r** Christopher Drake/house designed by Angela A'Court (orangedawe@hotmail.com); **91a** Alan Williams/Louise Robbins' house; **91b** Mark Scott; **92** Chris Everard/ Pemper & Rabiner home, designed by David Khouri, Comma (www.comma-nyc.com); **93a** James Merrell; **93b** Chris Everard/John Nicolson's house, London (johnnynicolson@aol.com); **94l** Henry Bourne; **94ar** Ray Main/Malin Iovino Design (iovino@btconnect.com); **94br** Christopher Drake/Nordic Style Kitchen (www.nordicstyle.biz); **95al** Polly Wreford/Foster House (www.beachstudios.co.uk); **95bl** Polly Wreford/ www.atlantabartlett.com; **95r** Polly Wreford; **96** Mark Scott; **97a** Dan Duchars/ Patrick Theis & Soraya Khan's home (www.theisandkhan.com); **97b** Debi Treloar/Michael Leva's home; **98** Christopher Drake/Maurizio Epifani's home (www.lorodeifarlocchi.com); **99a** Debi Treloar/Clare & David Mannix-Andrews' house; **99b** ph Andrew Wood; **100** Debi Treloar/Helle Høgsbro Krag's home (www.cremedelacremealaedgar.dk); **101al** & **ar** Debi Treloar/Anna Massee of Het Grote Avontuur's home (www.hetgroteavontuur.nl); **101cr** Henry Bourne; **101br** Tom Leighton; **102** Mark Scott; **103al** Debi Treloar; **103ar** Caroline Arber; **103br** Sandra Lane; **104 both** & **105al** David Brittain; **105bl** & **br** Sandra Lane; **105ar** Polly Wreford/ www.atlantabartlett.com; **106** David Britain; **107l** Polly Wreford/ www.atlantabartlett.com; **107r** Debi Treloar; **108** Mark Scott; **110l** Caroline Arber/Rosanna Dickinson's home; **110r** Christopher Drake/interior designer Vivien Lawrence (020 8209 0562); **111** Debi Treloar/Marcus Hewitt & Susan Hopper's home; **112** Chris Everard/Jeremy Hackett's house; **113a** Henry Bourne/designed by Charles Rutherfoord (www.charlesrutherfoord.net); **113b** Sandra Lane; **114** Christopher Drake/John Minshaw's house (www.johnminshawdesigns.com); **115a** Polly Wreford; **115b** Chris Everard/ designed by Helen Ellery of The Plot London; **116** Mark Scott; **118** Polly Wreford/Foster House (www. beachstudios.co.uk); **119al** Polly Wreford/designed by Belmont Freeman Architects (www. belmontfreeman.com); **119ar** David Montgomery; **119b** Polly Wreford; **120bl** Polly Wreford/Lena Proudlock's house (www.lenaproudlock.com); **120ar** Polly Wreford; **120br** Mark Scott; **121** Mark Scott; **122a** Jan Baldwin/ New York house designed by Brendan Coburn & Joseph Smith (www.coburnarchitecture.com); **122b** ph Debi Treloar/Petra Boase's home (www.petraboase.com); **123al** Debi Treloar/Susan Cropper; **123b** Polly Wreford/ Sasha Waddell's home (www.beachstudios.co.uk/ www.sashawaddelldesign.com); **123ar** Mark Scott; **124** Debi Treloar/Cristine Tholstrup Hermansen & Helge Drenck's house, Copenhagen; **125al** CICO; **125ar** Mark Scott; **125b** Polly Wreford/Foster House (www.beachstudios.co.uk); **126l** Sandra Lane/Harriet Scott's apartment (www.rkalliston.com); **126r** Winfried Heinze; **127al** Winfried Heinze/Jon Pellicoro's home (jpellicoro@earthlink.net); **127ar** Christopher Drake/Florence Lim's house, architecture by Voon Wong Architects (www.voon-benson.com), interior design by Florence Lim Design; **127br** Claire Richardson/Ann Louise Roswald's home (www.annlouiseroswald.com); **128** Henry Bourne; **129al** Caroline Arber; **129cl** Polly Wreford; **129bl** David Montgomery; **129ar** Winfried Heinze; **129cr** Polly Wreford; **129br** Henry Bourne; **130** James Merrell; **132** Debi Treloar/Marcus Hewitt & Susan Hopper's home, Connecticut; **133l** Christopher Drake/Maurizio Epifani's home (www.lorodeifarlocchi.com); **133r** Winfried Heinze/ Marsden home, designed by Kim Quazi (info@acq-architects.com); **134** Chris Tubbs/Julia & Michael Pruskin's home (Pruskin Gallery, London, 020 7937 1994); **135al** Winfried Heinze; **135ar** Winfried Heinze/interior architecture: matali crasset (www.matalicrasset.com); **135b** Debi Treloar/Mark & Sally Bailey's house (www.baileyshomeandgarden.com); **136l** Dan Duchars/Susan Cropper; **136ar** Andrew Wood/Roger Oates (www.rogeroates.com); **136br** Debi Treloar/Susan Cropper; **136a** Polly Wreford/Foster House (www.beachstudios.co.uk); **137b** Jan Baldwin/Sophie Eadie's home (www.tnesc.co.uk);**138** Jan Baldwin/Claire Haithwaite & Dean Maryon's home, Amsterdam; **139l** Chris Tubbs/Ben Pentreath's Georgian flat, Bloomsbury (www.working-group.co.uk); **139r** CICO; **140** Polly Wreford; **141a** Winfried Heinze; **141bl** Chris Everard; **141bc** Tom Leighton; **141br** Polly Wreford/Hilary Robertson & Alistair McGowan; **142** Chris Everard/NY apartment, designed by Mullman Seidman Architects (www.mullmanseidman.com); **144** Polly Wreford/Foster House (www.beachstudios.co.uk); **145l** Chris Everard/architect Jonathan Clark's home (www.jonathanclarkarchitects.co.uk); **145r** Polly Wreford/Clare Nash; **146l** Tom Leighton; **146r** Polly Wreford/Foster House (www.beachstudios.co.uk); **147l** Polly Wreford/ www.atlantabartlett.com; **147ar** Debi Treloar/Clare & David Mannix-Andrews' house; **147br** Debi Treloar/Jette Arendal Winther & Niels Winther's home (www.arendal-ceramics.com); **148** Henry Bourne; **149al** Polly Wreford/ home of Reinhard & Bele Weiss, London (www.3sarchitects.com); **149ar** Paul Ryan/ www.meterarkitektur.se; **149b** Christopher Drake/Suze Orman's NY apartment, designed by Mullman Seidman Architects (www.mullmanseidman.com); **150** Polly Wreford/Francesca Mills' house, London; **151al** Polly Wreford/ www.atlantabartlett.com; **151b** Polly Wreford/Abigail Ahern's home, London (www.atelierabigailahern.com); **151ar** Christopher Drake/Nordic Style bedroom (www.nordicstyle.biz); **151cr** Debi Treloar/Patty Collister's home (www.anangelatmytable.com); **151br** Chris Everard; **152a** Winfried Heinze; **152c** Debi Treloar/ Lena Renkel Eriksson (www.theswedishchair.com); **152b** Chris Everard; **153** Caroline Arber.

Jacket photographs:

Front jacket David Loftus. **Back jacket above left** Debi Treloar/Cristine Tholstrup Hermansen & Helge Drenck's house, Copenhagen; **above center** CICO; **above right** Debi Treloar/Clare & David Mannix-Andrews' house, East Sussex; **below left** CICO; below center Debi Treloar; **below right** Debi Treloar/www.baileyshomeandgarden.com; **spine** CICO.